My First Step in Crypto and Bitcoin Investing for Kids and Beginners

Simplified Introduction of Cryptocurrencies for Dummies

Sweet Smart Books

© Copyright 2021 - All rights reserved.

The content contained within this book may not be reproduced, duplicated or transmitted without direct written permission from the author or the publisher.

Under no circumstances will any blame or legal responsibility be held against the publisher, or author, for any damages, reparation, or monetary loss due to the information contained within this book, either directly or indirectly.

Legal Notice:

This book is copyright protected. It is only for personal use. You cannot amend, distribute, sell, use, quote or paraphrase any part, or the content within this book, without the consent of the author or publisher.

Disclaimer Notice:

Please note the information contained within this document is for educational and entertainment purposes only. All effort has been executed to present accurate, up to date, reliable, complete information. No warranties of any kind are declared or implied. Readers acknowledge that the author is not engaged in the rendering of legal, financial, medical or professional advice. The content within this book has been derived from various sources. Please consult a licensed professional before attempting any techniques outlined in this book.

By reading this document, the reader agrees that under no circumstances is the author responsible for any losses, direct or indirect, that are incurred as a result of the use of the information contained within this document, including, but not limited to, errors, omissions, or inaccuracies.

Table of Contents

Introduction 14
   Understanding the Importance of Decentralization 15
   Different Transaction Systems 16
      Barter System 16
      Commodity Currency 17
      Fiat Currencies 17
      Digital Currencies 17
      Cryptocurrencies 18

Chapter 1: Understanding Money 1
   Properties of Money 3
      Why is Trust Important for Currencies? 4
   Decentralized Currencies vs. Centralized Currencies 5
   What Is Investing? 5
      Different Types of Investments 6
         Silver, Gold, and Diamonds 6
         Real Estate 6
         Buying and Selling Products 7
         Opening a Business 7
         Stocks 7

Bonds 7

Mutual Funds 8

CDs 8

ETFs 8

Cryptocurrencies 8

Why Is Investing Crucial for an Individual? 9

    1. Provides Financial Independence 9

    2. Safe Retirement 9

    3. Higher Returns 9

    4. To Manage Taxes Efficiently 10

    5. Beat Inflation 10

Chapter 2: Understanding Cryptocurrencies 11

What Are Cryptocurrencies? 12

What Is the Double-Spending Problem? 12

A Real-World Example of the Usage of Cryptocurrencies 14

    Hashing 14

        What Is a Hash? 15

        Limitations With Hashing 16

    Consensus Mechanism 16

    Peer to Peer Network 17

Properties of a Blockchain System 18
    1. Immutable 18
    2. Decentralized 19
    3. Distributed 19
    4. Irreversible 19
    5. Resilient 20
    6. Transparent 20
    7. Pseudonymous 21

Consensus Mechanism and Cryptocurrency Mining 21
    1. Proof of Work 22
    2. Proof of Stake 22
    3. Proof of Authority 23

Chapter 3: Bitcoin and its impact 24

Understanding Bitcoin 25

Bitcoin History 26

Bitcoin Mining and Proof of Work Algorithm 27

    How to Start With Cryptocurrency Mining? 28

    Bitcoin Halving 28

Why Should Bitcoin Be Your First Choice? 29

Understanding How to Make a Bitcoin Transaction 30

    Roadmap to Make First BTC Transaction 31

1. Download Bitcoin Core 31
2. Download Bitcoin Wallets 31
3. Buy Bitcoin 33
4. Sending Bitcoin 33
5. Confirming Your Transaction 34

Understanding Keys and Addresses 34

How Is a Private Key Generated? 35

How Is a Public Key Generated? 35

Environmental Effects Due to Bitcoin Mining 36

Chapter 4: Fiat currencies Vs Cryptocurrencies 37

What Are Fiat Currencies? 38

Characteristics of a Fiat Currency 39

1. Controlled by a Centralized Institution 39
2. It Needs to Be Durable 39
1. It Needs to Be Portable 39
2. It Needs to Be Uniform 40
3. It Needs to Have a Limited Supply 40
4. It Needs to Be Divisible 40

How Are Fiat Currencies Traded? 40

Understanding Us Dollar-Pegged Cryptocurrencies 41

Tether and Its Importance 42

Chapter 5: Investing In Cryptocurrencies 43

- Understanding Cryptocurrency Brokers 44
- Understanding Cryptocurrency Exchanges 45
  - How to Choose a Cryptocurrency Exchange? 45
    1. Reliability and Authenticity 45
    2. Withdraw and Deposit Options 46
    3. Easy UI and Mobile Apps 46
    4. Great Customer Service 46
    5. Better Commission Rates 46
- Investment Strategies 47
- Popular Investing Strategies for Cryptocurrency 48
  1. Invest in Icos 48
     - How to Evaluate ICOs? 48
  2. HODL 49
  3. By Earning Yield 49
  4. Dollar-Cost Averaging 50
  5. Lump-Sum Investing 50
  6. Value Investing 51
  7. Value Averaging 51
  8. Contrarian Investing 52
  9. Growth Investing Strategy 52

10. Long/Short Strategy 52

Bears and Bulls in the Market 53

    A Bull Market in Depth 53

    A Bear Market in Depth 54

Technical Analysis 54

    Example for Technical Analysis 55

        Step 1: Learn About Different Charts. 55

        Step 2: Learn About Different Technical Indicators. 55

        Step 3: Master Support - Resistance Line 56

        Step 4: Mastering Trend and Chart Patterns ... 56

Fundamental Analysis 56

    Step 1: Analyze Financial Metrics. 57

        1. Market Capitalization 57

        2. Liquidity and Volume 58

    Step 2: Analyze Project Metrics 58

        1. White Paper 58

        2. Founder and the Team 58

        3. Competitors 58

        4. Tokenomics 59

    Step 3: Analyse Blockchain on-Chain Metrics 59

1. Active Addresses 59
2. Transaction Value 59
3. Transaction Count 60
4. Fees Paid 60
5. Hash Rate 60

Chapter 6: Future Of Cryptocurrencies 61

Applications of Blockchain Technology 62
1. Internet of Things 62
2. Money Transfer 63
3. Changing the World With Smart Contracts . 63
4. Blockchain Technology for Health Care 64
5. Blockchain Technology for Logistics 64
6. Art Collection With NFTs 65
7. Blockchain for Government 65
8. Blockchain Technology for Media 66

NFTs and Why They Are the Next Digital Revolution? .. 66

How Does an NFT Work? 66

ICOs and Future 67

Different Countries and Regulations 69

Cryptocurrencies for Crime and Theft 70

Chapter 7: Cryptocurrency Risks 71

What Are the Risks of Cryptocurrencies? 72

Risk Management 73

    Position Sizing 73

        Enter Amount vs. Risk Amount 74

        Elder's "Sharks" and "Piranhas." 74

        Kelly Criterion 75

    Risk / Reward Ratio 75

    Utilizing Stop Losses and Take Profits 76

Hedging for Avoiding Cryptocurrency Risk 76

    1.   Short Selling 77

    2.   Futures 78

    3.   Options 78

Chapter 8: Money Management And Saving 79

How to Save Money? 80

Money Management Techniques 82

Understanding Online Banking 83

Time, Patience, and Persistence For Investors 84

    Time 84

        How to Utilize Your Time Perfectly? 84

    Patience 85

    Persistence 85

Chapter 9: Everything about altcoins 87

Why Are Altcoins Vital? 88

How to Invest in Altcoins? 88

Ethereum and Its Importance 91

How Does Ethereum Work? 91

How Do These Decentralized Applications Work? 91

How Do Smart Contracts Work? 92

Cardano and Its Importance 93

How Does Proof of Stake Work? 93

Polkadot and Its Importance 94

How Does Polkadot Work? 94

Chain Link and Its Importance 95

Litecoin and Its Importance 96

Ripple and Its Importance 96

Why Is Ripple Necessary? 97

What Happens in a Ripple Net Transaction? 97

Chapter 10: Cryptocurrencies Vs Stocks 98

Understanding the Stock Market 99

What Is a Stock? 99

How to Invest in Stocks? 100

1. Using Online Brokers 100

2. Using Robo Advisers 101

3. Using Mutual Funds 101

How Are Stocks Different From Cryptocurrencies? 102

1. Volatility and Liquidity 102

2. Returns 102

3. Large Diversity 103

Advantages of Stocks 103

1. Gains 103

2. Drives a Growing Economy 103

3. Beat inflation 103

4. Dividends 104

Disadvantages of Stocks 104

1. Risky 104

2. Problems of Bankruptcy 104

3. Requires High Knowledge 105

Investing in Both Stocks and Cryptocurrencies 105

Different Types of Traders in the Financial Market 105

Day Trader 105

1. Swing Trader 106

2. Position Trader 107

3. Reverse Trader 107

4. Derivatives Trader 107

5. Scalper 108

Conclusion 109

Character Traits for Cryptocurrency Investors 109

References 113

Introduction

Bitcoin and all other cryptocurrencies are having a wild run in 2021. In April of 2021, the price of Bitcoin reached a high of $64000, making everyone in the financial world discuss its future and potential. All cryptocurrencies, however, had a steep fall when Elon Musk, the CEO of Tesla and a long term outspoken supporter of cryptocurrencies, tweeted citing the environmental effects of Bitcoin mining as the reason for removing it as a payment option for Tesla Cars after one year. Within a few days, Bitcoin and other cryptocurrencies lost their value by over 30%. Since then, investors and financial experts have been discussing the profits and volatility of cryptocurrencies from a larger perspective. Irrespective of these hurdles, in the second half of 2021, Bitcoin has reclaimed its previous price value and is currently close to $50,000.

Bitcoin and the underlying blockchain technology are the next life-changing innovation of humanity. This book helps beginners and kids understand the complex topics of cryptocurrencies in a simple way. The book's author focuses on delivering complex basics about cryptocurrencies and money management in general for a wannabe investor. To understand the different topics mentioned in this book, a reader must understand the importance of decentralization, the goal of cryptocurrencies, and the importance of Blockchain technology.

Understanding the Importance of Decentralization

In 2008, the world went through a recession phase due to the housing bubble crisis in the US residential housing market. Because the United States has the largest economy globally, the housing bubble crisis affected all countries directly or indirectly. People lost homes, jobs, and their lifelong savings. The main culprit for this recession is banks, which were not transparent in what they were doing. Even though they were the culprits, the United States' government bailed them out and helped them recover from their losses. In the end, banks' clientele lost their savings because of the negligence of centralized institutions.

In simple words, all banks, monetary governments, and reserve banks are centralized institutions that control anything related to finance. Centralization is everywhere globally, and is highly significant in the financial arena.

During this time a white paper sent in a cryptographic mailing list sparked a discussion in internet forums. The white paper, written by unknown entity Satoshi Nakamoto, claimed they found a solution for the double spending problem that stood as a hurdle for digital currencies.

Many were unenthusiastic about its implementation, but soon it started a revolution among technical and financial enthusiasts. After a decade, Bitcoin, mentioned in the white paper, has become a weapon for investors who thrive on decentralization and the technology built upon this ideology.

In simple words, anything that is not controlled by a single entity and provides power to everyone involved is called a decentralized system. Cryptocurrencies and the Blockchain technology that supports them are the major decentralized systems that exist in the world.

To understand in-depth about currency, you need to first learn about different transaction systems that thrived in our world during different timeframes.

Different Transaction Systems

World and Humans have used different ways to make transactions right from our inception. Our ability to understand the concept of value and use it for specific transactions has made us primitive among all other species in the world. Understanding different transaction systems humans have used during different times in the evolution of society is vital for appreciating the concept of decentralization and cryptocurrencies that facilitate it.

Barter System

The barter system is the first transaction system that civilized humans used. Researchers have dated it back as far as Mayan civilizations, where citizens effectively used barter.

In a barter system, two parties involved in the transaction exchange items of the same value. For example, if you have two bags of rice, you might exchange it with a cobbler for a new pair of shoes. The problem with the barter system is it becomes complex when it extends to a large community. Also, it is not entirely logical as people may have rice but not need shoes.

Commodity Currency

The barter system was soon replaced by commodity currency in all the flourishing civilizations, including as Mesopotamian, Egypt, and Harappa. Precious commodities such as gold, silver, and diamonds are used while buying or exchanging items. Though silver is popular, gold has been the most popular commodity for exchanges for a long time.

While commodity currencies are considered better than the barter system, it has become inconvenient for individuals to carry them all the time. They are heavy and are also not uniform.

Fiat Currencies

All the problems with commodity currency started to fade away when banks began to provide banknotes for individuals who stored commodities such as gold in their reserves. People trusted banknotes when banks released them as an easy way to make transactions. With the success of this system, banks soon started to distribute banknotes without taking any gold into their reserves from citizens. Soon, these banknotes have turned into fiat currencies and are now being used by citizens of different currencies in the world.

USD, CAD, and EUR are some of the popular fiat currencies in the world right now.

Digital Currencies

With the inception of the internet, the concept of digital ledgers became popular. Instead of transacting with paper notes, people started to exchange money using digital currencies.

Banks will update the user's ledger balance instantly whenever a transaction happens with a digital currency.

Companies such as PayPal and Payoneer have created a whole new payment mechanism to transfer money between businesses by providing assured protection. Digital currencies, however, are centralized and are controlled by a single entity, therefore every record can be monitored by government authorities if they want to. All digital currency platforms are also prone to hacking and can be a severe problem to individuals who don't follow simple security guidelines.

Cryptocurrencies

Cryptocurrencies are decentralized currencies that individuals can transact from one party to another without being monitored or controlled by a regulatory body. Cryptocurrencies are also difficult to hack and cannot be deleted or modified once entered into the blockchain system.

Every transaction system has its own merits and flaws, and as a crypto enthusiast, you must understand both the risks and rewards they provide. The book's author is determined to provide enough information that can help you judge both rewards and risks associated with different cryptocurrencies.

How to Use This Book?

This book focuses on delivering complex cryptocurrency topics in a simple way for beginners. Usage of varied examples, real-life concepts can help both kids and adults unfamiliar with the subject understand the essence that is important from a bigger picture.

We suggest using mind-maps or other cognitive techniques such as passive recall to consume the knowledge efficiently.

Why We Wrote This Book?

The ongoing Bitcoin run has made many individuals interested in it. Even though many books are available for the topic, most of them were overwhelming as they use complex terms unfamiliar to a layman. This book focuses on delivering the required content for wannabe crypto enthusiasts in an easier way.

Answer the questions in this checklist:

- Are you in debt?
- What is your primary goal for investing in cryptocurrencies?
- What is your capital?
- Are you enthusiastic about cryptocurrency, or are you just doing it for quick returns?
- Did you have trading experience before with any financial instruments?

Chapter 1:
Understanding Money

Humans used the barter system for thousands of years until they discovered it was inefficient to make transactions. Usage of commodity money dates back to ancient civilizations such as Harappa and Mesopotamian. Humans later improvised commodity money into representative money and started to accept it as a mode of transaction. This chapter focuses on delivering these topics in a simple way for beginners and experienced investors alike.

What Is Money? We use money for everyday transactions, either for buying products or to pay for services. Money is an item that is accepted as a payment choice worldwide in different designations known as currencies. For example, citizens use USD to make their daily transactions in the United States, whereas in Great Britain, citizens use GBP to perform their transactions.

Money can be termed as an intermediate for the exchange of both products and services. Money has different properties that have made it a preferred medium of exchange for hundreds of years since the fall of the inefficient medium of exchange systems such as barter and commodity transactions.

In the everyday world, we call money currency and generally accept it for all kinds of transactions, usually in a country. To become a valid currency, it should usually possess specific properties.

Properties of Money

1. People should easily be able to interchange it. If each currency unit is not interchangeable, it will become difficult to appreciate its value.
2. People should be able to use it as many times as possible. Durability helps currencies to participate in as many transactions as possible.
3. It should be easy to carry it from one place to another.
4. Everyone should know what you are giving to them. You can never use something as a currency if people don't trust it.
5. Its value should not fluctuate too fast. Having a stable value is essential for a currency to be trusted by all parties involved in the exchange.

The United States Dollar (USD) possesses all these properties and is considered a preferred currency by everyone in the international community. In comparison, the Venezuelan Dollar fluctuates highly due to high inflation and is not considered an excellent currency for transactions in the international community.

Exercise:

Find out both the top and bottom currencies in the world right now. Judge the importance of different currencies depending on the properties mentioned above.

Why is Trust Important for Currencies?

Anything in the world is considered valuable only if people place trust in it. For example, gold was deemed useful for decades because it can effectively conduct electricity and be used as a decorative item, whereas diamonds are considered beneficial because they are sharp and can be used to create dangerous warfare. Anything that has value will automatically gather trust from people.

Money is valuable because everyone in a community or a country uses it as a valid medium of exchange. People in a particular community or country trust a currency because it is issued by a centralized institution such as a Federal bank and is backed by a government.

Central banks that usually control the flow of a currency consider various degrees of investment practices to make the currency as stable as possible. The forex market, which is the largest financial market globally, is usually used for trading fiat currencies backed by governments.

Exercise:

Write a paper on why people cannot use the currency used in a board game such as Monopoly in the real world.

Decentralized Currencies vs. Centralized Currencies

Currencies are usually controlled by central banks of different countries with or without the help of governments. The value of fiat currency usually increases or decreases based on the reforms introduced by the government or policies implemented by these centralized institutions. The absolute power of centralized institutions makes it difficult for individuals to influence or make decisions that can help everyone involved in the system.

In a centralized system, power usually exists with a single entity and is not considered fair by economists and philosophers. The world is primarily centralized now. A centralized institution usually controls any service or product that you typically use. While the concept of centralization works well in many instances, it is considered not ideal by many, leading to the idea of decentralization.

In a decentralized system, absolute power doesn't exist with a single entity. Decentralized systems allow transparency and help to eliminate intermediaries, which usually cut down your profits. Regular fiat currencies such as USD, GBP, EUR are centralized currencies, whereas cryptocurrencies such as Bitcoin, Ethereum, Litecoin are decentralized currencies.

What Is Investing?

Investing is usually a process in which an individual allocates their money into a financial instrument with the hope of generating a passive income or a final profit. Investing has both risks and rewards determined by the performance of the financial instrument.

An individual who invests is known as an investor. An investor often tries to improve his returns by maintaining a diversified portfolio that extends to different types of investments. Investing is a preferred way by various financial enthusiasts to improve their savings. Every investment type has its own merits, demerits, risk, and reward factors. However, in general, it is believed that an investment choice with high risk usually delivers high rewards and vice versa.

Different Types of Investments

Let's first look at some of the most common investments around the world.

Silver, Gold, and Diamonds

Usage of commodities as an investment is classic. Many households in both developing and underdeveloped countries use these commodities for their savings. All the civilizations of the world that flourished thousands of years ago used gold and silver as an exchange value. Gold is becoming scarce and is no longer considered a good investment choice due to its reduced profit margin.

Real Estate

Real estate is a popular investment for individuals who have a good grasp of local conditions. Real estate investment also needs excellent communication and networking skills to achieve the best results. For quick returns on investment, beginners are encouraged to invest in real estate companies or to involve themselves in crowdfunding of real estate buildings.

Buying and Selling Products

Even though the profit is minimal, buying a product and selling it after a fixed time or sometimes instantly is considered a successful investment strategy by many investors. Investors can use automobiles, electronic appliances, and luxury items such as art for this purpose.

Opening a Business

Opening a business using your capital can also be considered a type of investment. When you open and run a business, you are practically working for a return on investment. Your business can either succeed or fail depending on various factors and sometimes even luck.

While these are traditional financial investments, we will now discuss modern financial investments that can achieve individual financial independence over time.

Stocks

Stocks are financial instruments that provide investors with a share in the company. When you buy stock in a company, you become the owner of a part of the company. As stock price increases, your value in the company's market capitalization increases. Stocks are easy to get into, and there is a lot of information available for regular investors. The stock market can also become complex if you are involved in the market as a day or derivatives trader.

Bonds

Bonds are legal agreements of debt by a government or financial institution. Bonds are considered a safe investment as they provide consistent passive income. Both governments and corporations use bonds to borrow money. All these bonds are tradable assets.

Mutual Funds

The purpose of a mutual fund is to pool the money of a number of investors to create a fund that they can invest in similar or non-similar assets according to a decision made by an experienced manager in charge of the fund. Mutual funds are passive risk financial instruments that provide consistent returns. Mutual funds can be divided into different types based on your capital.

CDs

Certificate of Deposits (CDs) is a financial instrument that guarantees a particular interest according to your provided amount. CDs are low risk instruments that guarantee profits. However, CDs are considered a lazy way to invest as the banks will lock out your money until the mature period.

ETFs

Exchange Traded Funds (ETFs) are indexes of different sectors or industries available on the stock market. For example, you can trade an index that lists and averages the performance of all real estate companies. ETFs are a great way to invest if you focus on a single commodity, sector, or industry. ETFs also have significant tax regulations and are a favorable choice for thousands of retail investors worldwide.

Cryptocurrencies

Cryptocurrencies are the trending digital assets that can be transacted using the secured blockchain system. Cryptocurrencies are currently ruling the financial world with their innovation and focus on decentralized finance systems. The rise in NFTs and ICOs also helped cryptocurrencies grab a decent place in the financial world.

Why Is Investing Crucial for an Individual?

1. Provides Financial Independence

There is no other way that provides financial independence as investing provides. Investing in different financial instruments can help an individual achieve his life goals, such as buying a house or providing a good college education for children. The interest that comes with a mix of assets can also provide a steady passive income for an individual.

2. Safe Retirement

Retirement is a scary thought for many individuals. Usually, people rely on salaries to meet their primary and secondary needs. The thought of living without a consistent income and a small pension is a scary thought for most individuals. To help individuals meet their retirement needs, governments order employers to allot a part of the income they earn into a 410k savings account or a certificate of deposit with their retirement date as its maturity date.

Investing provides a golden opportunity for individuals who are worried about their retirement years. Investing in different financial instruments offers higher returns than any other plans that employees usually use.

3. Higher Returns

Investing in different financial instruments provides higher returns over time. For example, stocks offer more than double your investment within less than five years if you have performed sufficient fundamental research before investing.

4. To Manage Taxes Efficiently

Investing helps individuals deal with their taxation more efficiently. Different state and central governments also provide their citizens to file for IT returns for a part of their income if they have invested in financial instruments such as mutual funds, stocks, CDs, and 401k savings accounts.

5. Beat Inflation

Inflation is an economic concept that exists in a growing economy. With the economy's growth, the supply and demand ratio will change, making the value of currency decrease with time. For example, if you can buy a television for $100 in 2021, you need to buy it for $200 in 2031. With time, inflation increases, and your saved money in bank accounts or CDs will become less valuable. By investing, you are however saving yourself from potential inflation problems by obtaining returns that are higher than the inflation rate.

Chapter 2:

Understanding Cryptocurrencies

Cryptocurrencies are financial instruments that support decentralization. Bitcoin, Ethereum, Ripple, Cardano, and Dogecoin are popular cryptocurrencies that took the world by storm with their innovative implementation of blockchain technology. Understanding the foundational goals of cryptocurrencies is essential to appreciate their impact on the global financial market in the last decade.

What Are Cryptocurrencies?

A cryptocurrency is a digital currency that supports complex cryptographic principles and makes it impossible to counterfeit or double spend it. Most of the cryptocurrencies are decentralized and are hence independent or isolated, unlike fiat currencies which are usually regulated by centralized institutions such as central banks or sometimes by governments themselves.

Cryptocurrencies are only available in digital form, and it is easy to record these transactions using a distributed public ledger in the blockchain system.

What Is the Double-Spending Problem?

Right from the inception of the internet, many enthusiasts have tried to use digital currencies as a transaction medium. However, all of them failed in finding a way to counter the problem of double-spending.

To understand the problem of double-spending in digital currencies, read the below example.

Simon, Brave, and Tom are three best friends. One day they visited a bird sanctuary and had a good day. Brave has a camera, and so he took most of the photos during their short trip. They came back, and Simon opened his Instagram feed and saw that Brave had uploaded their photos. He downloaded those photos and posted them in his Instagram feed. Here, Simon has used the picture downloaded from Brave's feed. Now, he also opened his Twitter account and posted the same image. Now, Simon has double-spent the picture. Of course, no one will question or judge him because it is a personal photo.

Now, let us imagine a different situation. Simon, Brave, and Tom decided to create a digital currency named "Friends" that they can use among themselves. This digital currency consists of a hexadecimal integer that is randomly generated from custom software. Simon sent the same hexadecimal digital currency twice to both of their friends, just as he used the same picture twice. However, both Brave and Tom have judged him, saying that he is cheating his friends by sending the same money twice. Double spending is a problem whenever there is a currency transaction because a currency has a value in the real world, and hence it cannot be used more than one time by the sender.

In the years since the inception of digital currencies, the world has faced the hurdle of the double-spending problem. Companies and banks maintain an online ledger that automatically updates a bank account according to one's transactions to solve this problem. However, an online ledger system is inefficient and is centralized. To solve the double-spending problem, cryptocurrencies use a network of systems that use a consensus mechanism to ensure that the currency is not being spent twice.

A Real-World Example of the Usage of Cryptocurrencies

Ross is a network engineer at Stanford University. He was very excited when he first heard about the peer-to-peer network mechanism that cryptocurrencies use to validate transactions. To check how transactions worked in real-time, he installed Bitcoin payment software that automatically sends money to the sender he has chosen.

He visited an electronics shop accepting Bitcoin as payment and scanned the QR code for his $1200 purchase of a television. He was surprised when the Bitcoin payment software automatically recognized the payment provider's address and sent 0.025 Bitcoin from his account. The transaction happened almost as instant as a regular bank or Apple Pay transaction.

Ross decided to dig further into the mechanics of a blockchain transaction. He installed Bitcoin mining software and became a node in the Bitcoin network. After careful observation of the transaction pattern in the software, Ross understood the whole process. He divided it into three major sections to help him understand the complex mechanism of a transaction. All cryptocurrencies use the exact means to make their transactions get validated and become secured.

Hashing

All cryptocurrency transactions are placed in a block once they happen. A block usually consists of information—the kind of information stored in a block changes according to the blockchain platform. For example, Bitcoin just saves the sender, receiver address, and the number of coins in the transaction. In contrast, Ethereum can store additional information such as smart contracts and non-fungible tokens.

For example, let us assume that A makes a transaction of 0.025 BTC to B. Now, the system will add the following details to a block in the bitcoin blockchain.

1. mjftswWricJMfzG5gmcwabJ9Lzh7wKoAu - This is the sender's address

2. myFgwbSGg39cwcGPPpKuxPtAyDMGNzNVEa - This is the receiver's address

3. 0.025 BTC - Number of coins involved in the transaction

4. The address of the previous block

Based on the above information, the cryptographic algorithm will generate a hash. Bitcoin uses the SHA-256 hashing algorithm to generate a hash based on the information provided.

For example, a hash looks like

a5be525472d8a78b11ccf23369ccfe2f71731a7cabf6813e5319d635b3484a04

The blockchain system will use the hash mentioned above for the next block as the previous block's hash value is used for the present block. In a blockchain system, a block is connected to another, and hence if any information in a block is altered, the hash changes, making the blocks disconnect.

What Is a Hash?

A hash is a complex cryptographic algorithm that generates a code based on the information provided. You can compare it as a fingerprint according to real-world scenarios. When any information is manipulated, that particular hash address will change, and the hashes connected to it will become invalid.

Limitations With Hashing

While hashing is a secure cryptographic method, it is easy to break it with computer software that automatically generates and checks thousands of hashes per minute. To solve this limitation, cryptocurrency added an additional layer of security known as a consensus mechanism. Proof of work is the most popular consensus algorithm that Bitcoin uses.

Consensus Mechanism

Let's assume someone with high computing power has succeeded in cracking the hashing numbers. Now, can they manipulate the information in the blocks? It is extremely unlikely because all cryptocurrencies use a consensus mechanism to validate a transaction.

For example, the Bitcoin blockchain uses a proof of work algorithm that asks the verifiers to solve complex mathematical problems. This verification usually takes ten minutes, and only then you can proceed to the next block. Waiting ten minutes for every block to change its hashing information is difficult for any hacker. Hence, blockchain makes sure that your transactions are legit and secure by combining hashing and a consensus mechanism.

Peer to Peer Network

Next, let's assume that someone with an incredible intellect and resources has succeeded in hacking the hashes and found a way and enough time to approve a consensus mechanism for all the blocks in the chain. Is it now possible to manipulate the data in a cryptocurrency?

It is highly unlikely because the blockchain technology that cryptocurrencies depend on usually exists as a peer-to-peer network instead of a centralized authority. In a peer-to-peer network, all the blockchain data will exist with several other nodes in the network. All these nodes usually sync their data automatically and approve their consensus to add a block in the chain. So, even if you have succeeded in hacking and completing the proof of work for a node, you still need to achieve it with 50% of other nodes to manipulate the data successfully.

This famous attack is termed a 51% attack, which is practically impossible in any popular cryptocurrency platform.

Properties of a Blockchain System

Even though blockchain technology was invented in the 1990s, it got popular only with the success of Bitcoin as a digital currency. With sufficient research and enthusiastic developers, we are now so close to implementing the real prowess of blockchain technology in real-world applications. Understanding some of the properties that have made blockchain technology be hailed as the next most significant invention after the Internet is an essential prerequisite for a crypto enthusiast.

1. Immutable

An immutable object is one that doesn't change after being created. All cryptocurrencies and blockchain technology support immutability. If a block is entered into a blockchain it cannot be manipulated, replaced, or falsified in any way. Doing so is impossible as blockchain technology uses a combined model of hashing, consensus mechanism, and decentralized peer-to-peer network structure. Immutability also provides high integrity and transparency.

For example, if Sam sends 0.54BTC to Tom, that particular transaction will forever stay on the blockchain, making it visible to anyone who wants to verify it. An individual can use tools such as Block Explorer to check transactions with a simple mouse click. However, remember that even though hailed as immutable, blockchain technology can still be defeated with a 51% attack. However, this kind of attack is considered impractical right now, according to several financial experts.

2. Decentralized

Cryptocurrencies primarily follow the model of decentralization to make essential decisions in the blockchain ecosystem. If a system is decentralized, then the ultimate power doesn't lie with a central authority but a little with everyone involved in the system. For example, from a technical point of view, every node has equal power over the blockchain in a blockchain system.

However, it is essential to remember that not every cryptocurrency that uses a blockchain system is decentralized. Cryptocurrencies such as Ripple are centralized and are controlled by a single authority. While there is a debate about whether or not it is better to believe in decentralized societies, every investor should choose whether or not to be involved in a decentralized financial medium.

3. Distributed

All cryptocurrencies depend upon distributed technology to verify, validate and store transactions on the blockchain. All the nodes in a blockchain platform store a distributed ledger that consists of all the transactions that ever happened on the platform. All the nodes involved receive rewards for existing in a distributed system that constantly verifies the digital signature of the transactions.

4. Irreversible

All cryptocurrencies support irreversible transactions. Once a transaction is made, verified, added to a block, and inserted into a blockchain, then anyone cannot reverse that particular transaction. Irreversibility eliminates scams and fraud. No centralized authorities such as the FBI or police can help you reverse a transaction once made. Even though irreversibility is impossible, it is essential to wait for six confirmations when a block is added to ensure that your transaction cannot be tampered with in any way. The characteristic of irreversibility also eliminates the double-spending problem that haunted digital currencies for decades.

5. Resilient

Cryptocurrencies are generally resilient in nature. Any natural calamities or ban cannot decrease the value of cryptocurrencies such as Bitcoin. Short-term problems such as power shortages cannot affect cryptocurrencies because nodes in the network usually extend overall geographical locations. Over the last decade, cryptocurrencies such as Bitcoin and Ethereum have shown their highly resilient nature irrespective of speculation, controversies, China's aggressive approach towards cryptocurrencies, and environmental concerns.

6. Transparent

Cryptocurrencies are highly transparent in nature. You can check any transaction that ever happened on the blockchain using a simple tool such as block explorer. Any hacking attack can be easily observed as all the stolen funds can be seen flowing in the blockchain itself. Understanding how to utilize the transparency cryptocurrencies provide is vital for a crypto enthusiast.

7. *Pseudonymous*

Many beginners mistake cryptocurrencies as entirely anonymous. Cryptocurrencies, however, are pseudonymous as it is pretty easy to look at all of your transactions if an attacker knows about your public address and identity. However, without a public address, it is difficult for an attacker to find your transactions and link them to your real-life identity.

Reports say that an average investor can be easily tricked or phished to reveal their real-life identity when a hacker attempts to hack their cryptocurrency wallet.

Consensus Mechanism and Cryptocurrency Mining

Centralized systems such as banks or payment providers use an online ledger to ensure that every transaction is trustworthy and honest.

For example, if A sends B $500, the bank servers will instantly update the ledger. All online ledgers usually have a public account number and a password that can approve a transaction. While these online ledgers are effective, they are less secure and restrict users from making certain transactions.

In decentralized systems where there are no centralized authorities to check whether or not a transaction is legit, the transactions are verified using a consensus mechanism.

1. Proof of Work

Proof of work is a concept that programmers first introduced in the 1990s to counter DDOS attacks and spam emails. It, however, remained unused until Satoshi Nakamoto used it as a consensus algorithm for Bitcoin in 2009. In a proof of work algorithm, miners in the network usually compete against each other to solve computational puzzles. These computational puzzles typically require high computational power to solve. Hence, miners with high-performing hardware can quickly solve the problem and broadcast the block to the blockchain. Once a block is broadcasted into the network, all other nodes in the network will verify the transaction, and once it is confirmed, the block will be added to the blockchain, and a reward will be given to the miner.

2. Proof of Stake

Proof of stake was developed in 2011 to counter the environmental problems that the proof of work consensus algorithm is criticized for. Proof of stake algorithm usually uses a pseudo-random selection process to become the validator for the next block. This random selection process usually depends on factors such as stake age, randomization, and node wealth. To increase your chances of becoming the validator, you need to look like a legit contributor to the blockchain.

Ethereum has recently announced the platform will completely adopt the proof of stake algorithm as the default consensus algorithm by 2022.

3. Proof of Authority

Proof of authority is a new consensus algorithm introduced in 2017 to overcome the limitations of proof of work and proof of stake algorithms. Vechain is a popular cryptocurrency that uses the proof of authority algorithm as its default consensus algorithm. In a proof of authority algorithm, all the validators who verify the transactions are pre-approved. Hence, there will be no election process to select the validator, saving time and resources.

Chapter 3:
Bitcoin and its impact

Bitcoin is the first decentralized cryptocurrency that took the world by storm in 2009. Bitcoin is loosely based upon the white paper that Satoshi Nakamoto published in the same year. The identity of the creator of Bitcoin is still a mystery since Satoshi Nakamoto disappeared from the public eye a decade ago. Understanding Bitcoin, its principles, and its contribution to the cryptocurrency world are essential for a beginner interested in investing in different cryptocurrencies available now.

Understanding Bitcoin

Bitcoin is the first digital currency that provided a solution for the double-spending problem using its peer-to-peer technology. Until then, people depended on banks or private companies such as Paypal to make transactions. All the nodes that verify the transactions present in the bitcoin network are known as miners.

To understand, a bitcoin system consists of Nodes (miners or verifiers).

Why is this node needed?

To store all the bitcoin code and its blockchain on their local computer.

Why do nodes do this?

To provide trust to individuals who are willing to use Bitcoin as a transaction medium or as a storage value.

How do nodes do this?

To become a miner in the blockchain system, you have to download the mining software and download the entire blockchain into your system. The bitcoin blockchain size is now roughly around 400 GB. The size of the blockchain increases as new transactions happen.

Bitcoin History

While blockchain technology, which is essential for Bitcoin to function, was invented in the 1990s, it remained unused until Satoshi Nakamoto decided to use it to solve the double-spending problem for digital currencies. In 2008, on a cryptography mailing list, Satoshi Nakamoto posted a paper entitled " Bitcoin: The peer-to-peer payment system ". In 2009, Nakamoto mined the first block of Bitcoin, which is famously known as the genesis block.

In the real world, Bitcoins were first used in dark web websites and by hackers to make anonymous payments. Usage of Bitcoin by smugglers and hackers also gave a bad reputation to it in the initial days. However, the rapid knowledge provided by the enthusiastic crypto community made it popular with speculators from the Wall Street community.

Interest in individuals regarding its future made Bitcoin price increase rapidly over years. An increase in demand for Bitcoin mining as a passive income method also drove the price of Bitcoins. In the second half of 2021, Bitcoin, the price of one BTC is fluctuating between $40,000 and $50,000. Financial experts are divided into two sides when estimating the future of Bitcoin. Many Wall Street experts such as Warren Buffett call it a speculative bubble, whereas others call it a once in a lifetime opportunity for retail investors.

Bitcoin Mining and Proof of Work Algorithm

All the transactions in blockchain technology need to be verified using a consensus mechanism. A consensus mechanism is typically an agreement that all the nodes must accept in a network to add a transaction to the blockchain.

Different cryptocurrencies use different consensus mechanism models to verify their transactions. Bitcoin uses the famous "proof of work" algorithm to validate transactions and add them to the blockchain.

In a proof of work algorithm, a miner (a node in the network) usually downloads all the blockchain data and waits for his chance to add a particular transaction to a block.

The process is usually like this:

1. A bitcoin miner waits for a transaction to happen. The transaction can be any amount. From a miner and blockchain perspective, it is just one transaction.

2. To verify a transaction, a miner needs to solve a complex mathematical problem. Bitcoin mining software usually guesses the hashing algorithm randomly. The time taken for solving a mathematical problem is entirely random. However, the time for guessing the correct number can be reduced by using advanced computing hardware such as ASICS, which are specifically developed for mining purposes.

3. Once the problem is solved, the miner will wait for all other nodes in the network to accept it. Once other nodes in the network provide the consensus, the transaction

will be added to the blockchain. This process usually takes from approximately 30 minutes to two hours.

4. Miners usually receive a reward in the form of a transaction fee and Bitcoin for verifying the transactions on the blockchain.

How to Start With Cryptocurrency Mining?

Bitcoin mining is very tough as its demand has increased exponentially over the past decade. To start with cryptocurrency mining, you need expensive mining hardware such as ASICs specifically designed for Bitcoin mining. Solo mining has also become primarily obsolete as it is challenging to mine a block independently, unlike in the initial days. Because mining farms are becoming more prevalent, solo mining is considered an inefficient and impractical way to mine Bitcoin. To counter this problem, you can join mining pools by paying a small fee for your rewards.

Bitcoin Halving

Satoshi Nakamoto introduced the concept of Bitcoin Halving to control inflation in the Bitcoin market effectively. Roughly every four years, the Bitcoin system is designed so that the release of new bitcoins a miner can earn as a reward is halved. In 2009, the reward for each block was 50 BTC, but right now, in 2020, it has been reduced to 6.25 BTC. The concept of Bitcoin halving echoes the fact that Bitcoins demand will be high and supply will be low, making the price more elevated in the future. Cryptocurrencies such as Dogecoin support unlimited supply and are hence considered illogical from both economic and technological perspectives. To make something great, it needs to be scarce, and Bitcoin follows it.

In the possible 21 million bitcoins, 18 million bitcoins are already mined, making it difficult for miners to mine the last blocks present in the blockchain. Bitcoin halving also makes the hashing algorithm complex, requiring additional computation power to solve the mathematical problems needed for validating a transaction.

Why Should Bitcoin Be Your First Choice?

Even though there are many promising cryptocurrencies such as Ethereum and Ripple in the crypto world, Bitcoin is still considered the best bet for an investor because only Bitcoin follows the core goal of cryptocurrencies, that is to say decentralization with strict rules. Bitcoin is designed so that it becomes nearly impossible for anyone to exploit it according to their wish. The famous 51% attack is also almost impossible due to the sheer user base that Bitcoin has.

1. Largest User Base

The user base of Bitcoin extends all over the globe. The user base of Bitcoin is also most passionate and is constantly trying to use it for their transactions. The most extensive user base also makes it more trustable than other alternative cryptocurrencies. Due to high demand from users, the price is relatively stable compared to other cryptocurrencies except during black swan events related to the crypto industry.

2. **More Accredited**

Many multinational companies also accept Bitcoin as a payment provider. When new companies decide to adopt it as a payment provider, the demand for Bitcoin will grow exponentially.

3. **Bitcoin Is the Initiator of the Revolution**

The cryptocurrency revolution started when Satoshi Nakamoto used blockchain technology to create a virtual digital currency that solves the double-spending problem. No matter how complex and innovative cryptocurrency comes into the market, media coverage and popularity will lead to Bitcoin. Financially illiterate people unaware of the opportunities the crypto world offers will also choose Bitcoin as their cryptocurrency to increase their returns.

4. **Is More Transparent and Safe**

Unlike other popular cryptocurrencies, Bitcoin is more transparent and is not maintained by a single central figure. Satoshi Nakamoto disappeared from public view and never tried in a way to influence the price of Bitcoin. Bitcoin is also safer and secured from a technical point of view, with only one known vulnerability in its history.

Understanding How to Make a Bitcoin Transaction

A few days back, Sam read about Bitcoin and decided to invest a part of his money in his savings account in a cryptocurrency. With a ton of research, he decided that it is better to invest in

Bitcoin itself as it is less volatile and has a lot of potential in the future.

Sam, however, is very new to cryptocurrencies and has struggled a bit to convert his fiat money into Bitcoins. After skimming over the internet and watching several videos on YouTube, he finally succeeded in investing his money. Sam made a roadmap to make it easier for beginners like you to make their first transaction.

Roadmap to Make First BTC Transaction

1. Download Bitcoin Core

To understand how a Bitcoin transaction works and make one of your own, it is essential that you first download Bitcoin core. Bitcoin core is available for all operating systems and even for smartphones. When you successfully install and run the Bitcoin core on your computer, it will automatically connect to other computers connected to the same network. These computers in the network are commonly referred to as nodes. All the nodes in the network can communicate with each other.

When you open Bitcoin core for the first time, it will download the updated Blockchain from other nodes on your computer. The Blockchain size is now more than 400 GB, so you need to be patient while downloading it to your local computer. Make sure there is enough space to run the Bitcoin core program without interrupting the file download. Once the Blockchain is downloaded and verified, you can now make your transactions.

2. Download Bitcoin Wallets

While downloading Bitcoin core and downloading your own Blockchain is preferred, many don't have enough hard disk space to store the entire Blockchain. To help individuals with this problem, Bitcoin wallets are used. Bitcoin wallets allow you to send and receive Bitcoins without a complete copy of Blockchain. The only disadvantage with a wallet is that you are trusting another node to receive transaction information in the Blockchain. However, you need not worry because the most web, hardware, and offline wallets are from trusted sources. You can easily verify this wallet software using their SHA-256 encryption code.

Electrum, Samourai, and Green are some of the popular Bitcoin wallets to get started with. Make sure that you do sufficient research and confirm that the wallet software is entirely reliable by reading user reviews before choosing it for your transactions.

How Does a Wallet Work?

When you install wallet software of any kind, it will first generate a seed. A seed is a randomly generated list of 12 to 24 words that is unique and is not used by any other wallet in the world. Using this seed, the software will generate your wallet public addresses. All these addresses are public and can be sent by you to the other party in the transaction to receive bitcoins.

To send bitcoins, you need to use a private key. Every public address will have a private key, which is unique and only belongs to you. Private keys are highly confidential and should only be known by the owner of the bitcoins. Anyone who gets access to a private key can easily steal your bitcoins. Whenever you need to send bitcoin to others, you need to use your public address and your private key to generate a unique cryptographic hash.

3. Buy Bitcoin

Individuals can usually exchange Bitcoin for fiat currencies from someone they know in the real world. However, it is highly unlikely that you will find someone willing to trade them with you, as most Bitcoin users prefer to be anonymous about their cryptocurrency wealth. To counter this problem, many exchanges and services have popped up in the last decade to easily buy cryptocurrencies using fiat money such as the US Dollar.

Coinbase, Binance are some of the popular services out there. Please do complete research before purchasing Bitcoin or any other cryptocurrencies on the internet.

4. Sending Bitcoin

To send Bitcoin to someone with a public address, you need to use a Bitcoin wallet and enter the below-mentioned data.

1. Public address of the receiver

2. Amount of Bitcoin you wish to send to them

3. Fee for your transaction

You can click send and the transaction will be broadcast into the Bitcoin network right away.

What Happens When You Send Bitcoin?

At first, your transaction will be inserted into a block once initial verification is confirmed. Usually, several transactions are entered into a block instead of one. Initial verification will check whether or not you have sufficient BTC to send and generate a digital signature that can be used to verify whether or not your transaction is legit without revealing your private key.

Once verified, these groups of transactions in a block will be stored in a memory pool. A memory pool is a waiting area for new blocks that have been broadcast to the network. After 10 minutes, a node will choose your block and start broadcasting it to other nodes in the network after performing mining. Mining is entirely random and can take 10 minutes to a few hours to confirm your transaction.

You can attach an additional fee while making a transaction to improve your chance of mining your block with higher speed. From a technical point of view, however, mining is considered an entirely unpredictable system. The Blockchain system will usually reward the transaction fee the sender has paid to the miner.

5. Confirming Your Transaction

Once you have made a transaction, you need to use Blockchain tools such as Block explorer to check whether or not your transaction is confirmed. Not doing so will become a headache, especially when the sender pauses or reverses the transaction. When a transaction is in a memory pool, sometimes algorithms can cancel it due to network concerns.

Understanding Keys and Addresses

When you need to make an online transaction using your bank, you need to enter both your account number and your password. Banks also add additional security in the form of one time passwords and two-factor authentication.

Similarly, Bitcoin transactions use keys and addresses to make sure everything is secure. A public key in a cryptocurrency transaction is like your bank account number, whereas a private key is like a password.

How Is a Private Key Generated?

A private key is just a random number that is generated by the Bitcoin wallet software. However, this number is very long, so it is usually represented in a hexadecimal format to reduce its length. Private keys need to be kept secretly and safely. If you lose your private key, you are out of luck, and your Bitcoins will forever be locked out.

How Is a Public Key Generated?

A private key is usually used to generate a public key. Unlike a private key, bitcoin users can share the public key with anyone. All you need to do is use a mathematical function such as a hash to generate a public key so that other users cannot detect your private key. However, a public key is usually a very large number, and hence it becomes difficult to send it to other users in the network. To solve this problem, crypto analysts found an easy way to compress the key into a shorter form and called it an address.

For example,

5f01b70025c6895302c0fe44a049424c414f59a62db53c9bb1c8fcf4fe04e28e is a private key

0336970CE32E14DC06AC50217CDCF53E628B32810707080D6848D9C8D4BE9FE461 is a public key generated from the above private key

1PaBgxrA2MzdBvHSCUFh66PndKf3eXiBad is a compressed address of the above public key

Environmental Effects Due to Bitcoin Mining

Bitcoin's dependency on computational power to validate transactions has often been called one of the mainstream problems to become a replacement for fiat currency. Bitcoin also generates large quantities of e-waste, which directly contributes to global warming and climate change. While many crypto enthusiasts argue that more than 70% of the energy mining pools use renewable energy, it is not a valid argument.

In the last few years, energy used for cryptocurrency mining has surpassed the annual energy usage of small countries such as New Zealand and Romania. Many cryptocurrencies are trying to migrate to a proof of stake algorithm instead of using a proof of work algorithm to solve this problem. Green Cryptocurrencies such as Cardano and Stellar are right now in high demand with the crypto community due to their promise of delivering high-level smart contract platforms with minimal energy usage.

Chapter 4:

Fiat currencies Vs Cryptocurrencies

As a cryptocurrency investor, you must understand its counterpart fiat currencies. While cryptocurrencies are decentralized and are entirely dependent on blockchain technology, fiat currencies are centralized and issued by governments. Knowing the stark differences between both types of currencies and understanding how to use them effectively is a prerequisite for an ambitious investor.

What Are Fiat Currencies?

Fiat currency is government-issued money that is usually not backed by any commodity such as gold. Until fiat currencies were introduced, the world followed a monetary system known as the gold standard. In a gold standard monetary system, the value of currency depended on the gold reserves it held. Gold standard, however, became complex and was soon abolished by the United States government as USD was used as an official currency. Fiat money doesn't have intrinsic value but stays in a flow because it is declared legal tender by controlling centralized institutions.

Soon, fiat currencies and a foreign exchange market to control these currencies' exchange rate is established to maintain a better currency system. USD, EUR, and GBP are some of the popular fiat currencies. Fiat money is the main reason for the success of modern financial markets and the economic revolution in the mid-'90s.

Characteristics of a Fiat Currency

1. Controlled by a Centralized Institution

Every country uses its own central body to determine how many notes to be printed and how much currency needs to flow for a particular financial year, depending on the demand and supply for the currency. Even though absolute control of currency lies with centralized institutions, the currency's value is determined by the collective trust in it by individuals in that country. If citizens of the country lose faith in their country's currency, then its value tanks more. Venezuelan and Zimbabwean currency crises due to hyperinflation are excellent examples of these kinds of scenarios.

2. It Needs to Be Durable

All fiat currencies need to be durable. Their value should not increase or decrease suddenly. Very high fluctuations in the value of a currency don't make them durable. For example, due to hyperinflation, the Zimbabwean dollar has surpassed 1 million Zimbabwean dollars for a single US Dollar. All government bodies that issue and control the currency flow should ensure that inflation is at a limit.

1. It Needs to Be Portable

Fiat money should be portable. The failure of commodities currencies such as gold is mainly due to the fact of not being portable. With the help of credit cards, digital payment services, and online accounts, fiat money is now so portable.

2. It Needs to Be Uniform

Every designation of a fiat currency should be of the same value. That is, one USD of yours should be equal to one USD of mine. Without uniformity, a fiat currency cannot be trusted by individuals involved in a transaction.

3. It Needs to Have a Limited Supply

Inflation is a complex concept but holds a special significance in a country's economy. Inflation is primarily dependent on the supply and demand of different industries in the country. With an increase in unemployment and a decrease in the average median salary, inflation increases, and the prices of the products will increase. If governments print more currency to escape inflation, the currency value will decrease, making it valueless. Usually, central banks such as the Federal Reserve have a mechanism to control the currency supply.

4. It Needs to Be Divisible

To act as a unit of money that people can trust, any money should be divisible. For example, a $100 bill can be divided into hundred $1 bills and ten $10 bills. The most divisible unit is the minimum unit that can be used for transactions. For example, one cent is the smallest unit that can be used in a USD right now.

How Are Fiat Currencies Traded?

Usually, individuals can use fiat currencies issued in a country only in that particular country. For example, USD used in the United States is not valid in Great Britain, and GBP used in Great Britain is not valid in the United States. To exchange different fiat currencies, foreign exchange trading is preferred. The forex market is the largest financial market globally and directly influences and is dependent on the world economy.

All the fiat currencies are traded in pairs instead of as single assets in the forex market. For example, EUR/USD is a famous currency pair that is traded on the forex market. The forex market is speculative and involves big market players such as central banks, private banks, and multinational companies. Central banks use different strategies to make sure that the currency exchange rate doesn't decline drastically.

Understanding Us Dollar-Pegged Cryptocurrencies

USDT is a famous US dollar-pegged cryptocurrency that is used widely by crypto investors all around the world. A cryptocurrency pegged to a fiat currency such as USD is known as a pegged currency or a stable coin. A stable coin offers stability to an investor with the help of the reserves that it maintains.

The advantage of using a stable cryptocurrency for your transactions is that it is more secure due to the blockchain ecosystem. Investors primarily use stable coins to convert easily into fiat currency without worrying about exchanges' transaction fees and spreads.

Cryptocurrencies can also be pegged to commodities such as Gold and Silver. Out of all the pegged cryptocurrencies, Tether is the most popular one right now in the cryptocurrency market. One Tether USDT token is valued at one one US dollar.

All popular cryptocurrency exchanges provide Tether as an easy way to involve yourself in peer-to-peer trading.

Pegged cryptocurrencies, however, face many problems as it is often difficult to hold reserves and maintain a stable value because the market is volatile. Pegged cryptocurrencies are usually centralized, with an autonomous body looking over reserves and examining them to update the latest information for the community. Reliable communication is a key to the success of pegged cryptocurrency projects.

Tether and Its Importance

Tether is the most popular stable coin right now in the crypto world. All tether tokens are represented using the token symbol USDT. Tether works as an easy way to exchange cryptocurrencies without depending on the exchange rates of fiat currencies. Tether uses reserves as collateral to make its value stable. Some pegged currencies focus on using non-collateral methods to achieve stability.

The main focus of Tether as a cryptocurrency is to eliminate the bridge between cryptocurrencies and fiat currencies. However, remember that Tether doesn't guarantee to provide you with a valid exchange rate for fiat currencies when there is huge volatility in the market.

Chapter 5:
Investing In Cryptocurrencies

Investing in cryptocurrency needs a lot of determination, patience, and persistence. Unlike traditional stock markets, cryptocurrencies are traded 24 hours a day. Cryptocurrency markets can be considered liberal investment choices as they are highly volatile and fluctuate all the time. To succeed in cryptocurrency markets, an investor needs to know different trading disciplines, strategies, and philosophies.

Cryptocurrency investing and trading appear complicated for beginners but are just usually a mouse click away. The confusion about how to correctly invest in cryptocurrencies is mainly due to various exchanges and brokers in the market. For a beginner, it becomes extremely difficult to choose a reliable exchange or broker for their trades. Understanding the differences between brokers and exchanges and knowing whom to use is an important skill a crypto investor needs to have sound knowledge about.

Understanding Cryptocurrency Brokers

According to financial terms, an investment broker is an intermediary who provides individuals with different financial instruments in exchange for money. Usually, crypto investors buy or sell different cryptocurrencies by exchanging fiat currencies. Brokers are generally trusted and have large reserves to back their user requests. For a beginner, it is as simple as opening an account and funding their account to buy different cryptocurrencies. However, if you are buying large quantities, brokers cannot authorize your orders. Brokers are suitable for low-level investing and trading.

All brokers provide highly secured hardware wallets to store your cryptocurrencies and use them for spot trading. Many investors use brokers to involve themselves in peer-to-peer cryptocurrency trading. Bitpanda is a great cryptocurrency broker for beginners.

Understanding Cryptocurrency Exchanges

A cryptocurrency exchange usually directly links buyers and sellers to either sell or buy different cryptocurrencies. Cryptocurrency exchanges can be both centralized and decentralized. However, 90% of the crypto exchange market is centralized and needs all users to provide KYC compliance according to their country's regulations. A cryptocurrency exchange usually charges users for every trade. Cryptocurrency exchanges are a great way to participate in crypto speculation. Investors can easily liquidate their crypto positions into fiat currencies and withdraw them to their bank accounts.

How to Choose a Cryptocurrency Exchange?

There are hundreds of cryptocurrency exchanges in the market right now, and it usually becomes a headache for investors to choose one among them. We provide some of the important criteria that you need to look out for in a cryptocurrency exchange.

1. Reliability and Authenticity

Research about the reliability of the exchange and the time in which they usually clear their orders. Having a reliable cryptocurrency exchange is essential, especially during a volatile market. An investor also needs to research the authenticity of the exchange.

2. Withdraw and Deposit Options

A reliable cryptocurrency exchange should have a fast way to withdraw and deposit funds. It also should have various payment providers to deposit the amount into the trading account easily. Some of the popular payment providers that a cryptocurrency exchange needs to provide are PayPal, Payoneer, master, and Visa credit cards.

3. Easy UI and Mobile Apps

A cryptocurrency exchange needs to have a UI that provides a great user experience. While choosing a better user interface is entirely subjective, a good exchange platform usually provides a minimal interface to make the process easy. An exchange platform should also offer mobile apps for different operating systems such as Android and iOS.

4. Great Customer Service

For a cryptocurrency exchange to be a top in the industry, it needs to provide a fast and easy customer experience for the investor. A good exchange platform usually includes e-mail, phone, and video assistance for their users.

5. Better Commission Rates

Commission rates are entirely subjective according to the type of investing you usually do in the crypto market. For example, if you make more trades in a week, having a default commission rate is better. On the other hand, having a dynamic commission rate for trades is a better choice if you are a position trader and perform a few trades.

What Documents Do You Need for KYC Compliance?

- Social Security Number
- Scan of any Government Identification card
- Bank account details
- Credit score and tax details if applicable

Investment Strategies

An investment strategy is like a blueprint which beginners and experienced investors can use to get higher returns by following a set of instructions. These strategies, however, don't guarantee your returns but can reduce your risks when there is huge volatility. Investing strategies in cryptocurrency can be divided into different types based on their approach, risk, and returns. Strategies can also depend on your portfolio management and your overall asset value.

Why Is It Important to Have a Strategy?

- Strategies help investors be aware of different situations they may face down the road of an investment. Strategies are just a preparation for roadblocks that may occur in your journey.
- Strategies can help investors to make decisions more accurately based on the situation they are in.
- Following a strict strategy can also make investors not attracted to manipulative assets due to FOMO (Fear of missing out) or not become prey to dangerous activities such as panic selling and revenge trading.

- Strategies can help you reduce risks and ensure that you are not losing too much than you can afford.

- Strategies can help you set realistic goals to secure your wealth and have a fruitful career in finance and investments.

Popular Investing Strategies for Cryptocurrency

1. *Invest in Icos*

The crypto world is full of exciting new projects that can become mainstream cryptocurrencies in the coming years. Finding winners from a lot of new cryptocurrencies is a difficult task for an investor. When you invest in an ICO, you need to be sure to hold those tokens until their value is at least doubled.

How to Evaluate ICOs?

1. Use websites such as Cryptowatch to observe hundreds of new projects from different exchanges and observe the buying patterns of crypto investors. Understanding market forecasts and market psychology can help you greatly, especially when investing in a new project.

2. Read the white paper on ICO and judge the idea behind the project from different perspectives. A white paper is a document that all new projects use to define their goals, budget, and architecture.

3. Head over to the project's community and observe the enthusiastic levels of the community members. Research about the founders and the developers that are going to contribute to the project. Finding any popular blockchain developers on this list can be a great positive sign for the project.

4. Understand the coin distribution philosophy the project uses. Analyze the project's technical features. Make sure that the project supports the usage of smart contracts as it is essential these days.

5. Check whether or not they exist on different popular cryptocurrency exchanges such as Coinbase and Binance.

2. HODL

Most of the financial assets appreciate over time. For example, stocks such as Apple and Google have increased more than ten times their initial value. Popular cryptocurrencies are no different. HODL is an acronym for 'hold on for dear life'. In a HODL cryptocurrency strategy, all you have to do is buy the asset and keep it for years. Holding is fruitful and will give excellent results in any financial ecosystem.

3. By Earning Yield

Yield cryptocurrencies are quite similar to savings accounts that provide a particular interest for the money kept in the bank account. Yield cryptocurrencies are third-generation cryptocurrencies that are helping investors earn a passive income while holding their coins. Yield cryptocurrencies usually provide a great use case for decentralized financial applications requiring stake coins to validate transactions using a consensus mechanism.

4. Dollar-Cost Averaging

Dollar-cost averaging is an investment strategy where a crypto investor allocates a particular amount to invest in cryptocurrencies. For example, if an investor invests $100 every month in different diversified cryptocurrencies, it can be called a dollar-cost averaging strategy. With a dollar-cost averaging strategy, a crypto investor's main focus will be on long-term returns, and hence short-term fluctuations will not matter from a larger perspective.

5. Lump-Sum Investing

Lump-sum investing is a crypto strategy that is entirely contrary to the dollar-cost averaging method. In the lump-sum investing technique, an investor usually invests a large sum of money all at one time. Lump-sum investing is a strategy used by many investors for short-term gains. However, lump-sum investing is considered risky as there is a chance of a crash or bull run when you are holding your positions.

Instead of using the only method, a rational investor usually oscillates between lump sum and dollar-cost averaging methods according to their requirements.

6. Value Investing

Value investing is a popular investing strategy that was popularised by Warren Buffett. In a value investing crypto strategy, an investor usually needs to find an undervalued cryptocurrency at this moment and invest in it. Value investing requires a lot of research and patience for satisfactory results. Many value investors usually take years before they see any growth in their portfolio.

While researching for value investing, a crypto investor will usually believe in the core goal and approach of the company instead of deciding by factors such as volatility and liquidity that are generally dependent on market movement.

7. Value Averaging

Value averaging is mostly similar to value investing but with a characteristic difference. All the money you invest in an asset is dependent on different fundamental factors related to that asset. For example, if the asset is in a bearish cycle, the investor will invest more money into it and decrease his investment if the asset is in a bullish cycle.

Value averaging is often compared to the dollar average method due to their similarities of consistent money investment into an asset. However, value averaging is considered a liberal crypto strategy, whereas dollar cost average is a conservative method to make profits over the long term.

8. Contrarian Investing

A contrarian investor, most commonly known as a reverse trader, usually observes the market forecasts and does the opposite of what the majority was doing. For example, if the majority of the market is selling their positions, then a contrarian trader will buy more positions. However, being a contrarian is highly risky and needs a lot of patience as most of the time, it needs a long-term holding to get back your profits.

9. Growth Investing Strategy

In a growth investing strategy, an investor believes in cryptocurrencies and projects that are showing high growth. Investors involved in growth investing strategies usually look out for short-term returns. Cryptocurrencies such as Dogecoin are a great example of growth cryptocurrencies.

10. Long/Short Strategy

In a long strategy, an investor usually owns those stocks. In a short strategy, an investor doesn't own those stocks but owes them to other investors. All crypto investors can use the classic long/short technique to take advantage of undervalued and overvalued cryptocurrencies.

For example, if a crypto asset is undervalued, then investors will take a long position. On the other hand, if a crypto asset is overvalued, an investor will prefer to short the position. It would be best to use different technical and fundamental analysis techniques to determine when an asset is overvalued and undervalued.

Bears and Bulls in the Market

Bears and Bulls are two ways to describe market movement by financial enthusiasts. The usage of the words bears and bulls exists in every financial market. While the stock market popularised it, the crypto market also adopts the same principles when describing them.

The Crypto Market, when it is experiencing consistent growth, is known as a bull market, and a crypto market that is experiencing a consistent decline is known as a bear market.

A Bull Market in Depth

Bulls in the market drive the prices higher by buying more open positions in a cryptocurrency and increasing market confidence. In a bull market, an average retail investor is optimistic about the future of cryptocurrencies and their overall impact on the financial system. In a bull market, developers also will receive huge funding for their revolutionary cryptocurrency projects. Even though there are short-term fluctuations in a bull market, they are minimal and will not hurt the overall sentiments of the market.

However, bull markets are not permanent, and at some point, investors will lose their confidence and start to dump their positions. Market forecasts will suddenly influence the overall market, and the prices will decrease drastically, leading to a bear market.

A Bear Market in Depth

Bears in the market usually short their positions and wait for the prices to drop. When there is a bear market, the overall confidence of the market will decrease, leading to many unsuccessful projects or projects ending without any funding. Bears are usually experienced traders with high-value positions. During a bear market, it will be difficult for retail traders to make any profits.

The bear market usually occurs due to over-optimism or world events. In a cryptocurrency market, a bear market will usually occur due to influencers such as Elon Musk. For example, in May 2021, Elon Musk's statements on the environmental impact of cryptocurrencies led to cryptocurrencies tanking their value by 40%.

However, bear markets are not permanent either. Every time after a crash, new technologies and projects will lead to a bull market again.

Technical Analysis

Technical analysis is a popular trading discipline that investors use to predict the price movements of different financial instruments. Technical analysis became quite popular with stock investors in the last few decades. Crypto investors also depend on technical analysis to observe trends and utilize past price movements to predict the next price movements.

How Does Technical Analysis Work?

Technical analysts believe in the core goal of repeating itself. The technical analysis depends mainly on price and volume. When both price and volume are plotted in a chart, patterns will emerge, helping technical analysts to find repeating patterns easily. Using advanced chart patterns such as candlestick charts can simplify this task.

Technical analysts also believe in the supply and demand concept. Technical analysis is mainly considered as a better trading discipline for day traders. Both swing and position traders can also utilize technical analysis skills, but their impact decreases for long-term trades.

Example for Technical Analysis

Tom is a cryptocurrency trader who decided to use technical analysis as his preferred trading discipline. However, he is not yet fully aware of getting started and being proficient in using technical analysis. This section provides a step-by-step roadmap Tom can use to master technical analysis and predict price movements of different cryptocurrencies.

Step 1: Learn About Different Charts.

As a technical analyst, Tom needs first to master different kinds of charts that can be used to grasp how an asset is performing quickly. For example, bar charts and candlestick charts are the most popular charts for cryptocurrency investors.

Step 2: Learn About Different Technical Indicators.

Once Tom is proficient in reading different charts, he needs to learn about some popular technical indicators such as Relative strength index (RSI), Bolingbrook bands, Stochastics, and Moving average convergence divergence (MACD). All these technical indicators can be easily available using online chart tools. Technical indicators can help investors like Tom to detect patterns and anticipate future moves.

Step 3: Master Support - Resistance Line

The market usually experiences a tug of war between bulls and bears at a particular price level known as support-resistance level. As an investor's psychology generally determines the price of an asset during a short time, detecting a support-resistance line and finding a change in the trend is an important way to get some quick returns.

Step 4: Mastering Trend and Chart Patterns

During a price change, it is essential to predict exactly when a price reversal will happen. Tom finally should know about chart patterns such as pennants, double bottom, and Ascending triangles to master his technical analysis ability.

With sufficient knowledge of technical analysis, it is now time to learn another trading discipline called fundamental analysis to improve your trading skill set.

Fundamental Analysis

Fundamental analysis is a trading discipline where an investor measures the intrinsic value of a security asset by analyzing various economic and financial factors. Fundamental analysis can be applied to any financial instrument and is believed to be more difficult than technical analysis. Many investors, however, argue that fundamental analysis is a more accurate prediction technique than technical analysis. Wall Street big heads such as Warren Buffet only depend on highly researched fundamental analysis to make their trading decisions.

The goal of the fundamental analysis is to determine whether or not the current value of a financial instrument is of the right value. With cryptocurrencies, fundamental analysts use factors such as market capitalization and daily trade volume to determine the value of a crypto asset.

Example:

Tom is a crypto investor who decided to invest in an altcoin known as "Stellar." He chose to perform fundamental analysis on Stellar to determine whether or not it is a safe choice for an investment.

To make his fundamental analysis approach more straightforward and accurate, Tom divided the fundamental analysis into analyzing three metrics. An investor can use any of the below-mentioned metrics to determine the intrinsic value of a cryptocurrency.

Note: Unlike stock markets and other financial instruments, it is easy to find reports and metrics for different cryptocurrencies as the entire data is available in the blockchain itself. You may use public APIs or private APIs to look at the required metrics for efficient fundamental analysis.

Step 1: Analyze Financial Metrics.

Financial metrics describe the economic prospects and future of a cryptocurrency. Financial metrics are the popular metrics many fundamental analysts use to judge the performance of cryptocurrency and its blockchain ecosystem.

Important Financial Metrics:

1. Market Capitalization

Market capitalization is probably the most important financial metric to judge the performance or popularity of cryptocurrency in the market. However, it is difficult to determine how many tokens are in circulation based on this single financial metric.

2. Liquidity and Volume

The liquidity and volume of a cryptocurrency over time can help investors judge the historical performance of the cryptocurrency and predict future prices.

Step 2: Analyze Project Metrics

1. White Paper

A white paper is the single file that provides complete information about your cryptocurrency project. It is usually entirely technical and describes the goal of the project. Reading a white paper can help determine the overall focus and philosophy the founders follow. Technical details related to decentralization, licenses, tokens, and upgrades will also be usually determined with a white paper.

2. Founder and the Team

The success of a project can be determined by its founders and the team that works on it. Having talented blockchain developers on the team can make the process easier. Check their GitHub performance and popularity to find out their reliability for the project.

3. Competitors

To estimate the future of a cryptocurrency project, you also need to do careful research about their competitions. For example, Ethereum and Cardano both rely on providing smart contracts for decentralized applications. It would be best if you researched Ethereum and its development before investing in Cardano completely.

4. Tokenomics

Whenever a project is initiated, a white paper is released that consists of how the founders will distribute their tokens and the exchanges they are going to use. Tokenomics will also help you know about the consensus mechanism the founders will use for the project. For example, the Proof of Work (POW) algorithm is being criticized for its bad effect on the environment.

Step 3: Analyse Blockchain on-Chain Metrics

On-chain metrics are usually metrics that investors can easily observe from a block explorer or by using an API. Technical experts typically use On-chain metrics to analyze the performance of the blockchain platform. Several websites, such as CoinMarketCap, can provide a lot of blockchain information for a fundamental analyst.

1. Active Addresses

Calculating the number of addresses involved in a transaction can help fundamental analysts understand the popularity of the blockchain as a transaction medium.

2. Transaction Value

Fundamental analysts also check whether the transactions are higher or lower according to value. For example, 50 ETH is a smaller transaction, and 5000 ETH is a bigger transaction in terms of value. Daily transaction volume increases if the value of transactions is higher. High transaction value also means that the users of the platform are trusting the blockchain platform.

3. Transaction Count

Daily transaction count can act as a good measure of activity to judge the traffic of a network. However, make sure that the transactions are genuine and are not being transferred between their own wallets to manipulate the investors.

4. Fees Paid

The increase in the amount of fees paid can determine the demand for block space from investors.

5. Hash Rate

When there is a high demand for performing the consensus mechanism of transactions, the blockchain platforms are designed to increase the mechanism's hash rate. An increase in hash rate usually refers to the popularity of the cryptocurrency.

Chapter 6: Future Of Cryptocurrencies

Though they are volatile and unstable, cryptocurrencies are believed to be the next generation of the internet by many tech enthusiasts. The future of cryptocurrencies mostly depends upon how the world adapts to evolving blockchain technologies worldwide. With its growing popularity and developers showing interest in creating innovative decentralized applications, it is not an exaggeration to believe that blockchain technology will decentralize the world within the next hundred years. By understanding different applications of blockchain technology, we can easily judge the future of cryptocurrencies.

Applications of Blockchain Technology

Blockchain is a technology that extends its use cases across various domains, just like the internet. The wide range of applications that developers can build upon blockchain platforms usually follows decentralized principles. These decentralized principles and applications have the potential to revolutionize different sectors by eliminating intermediaries. Knowing some of the applications that Blockchain technology can aim for is a great way to understand the future Blockchain dreams about.

1. *Internet of Things*

The internet of things is usually criticized for safety concerns. However, with decentralized technology, all your data will be safe, and there is no way for hackers to manipulate or steal your data. Blockchain technology introduces higher-level security and also improves the scalability of IOT applications. Filament and HYPR are believed to be the next generational IOT companies that depend on blockchain technology.

2. Money Transfer

With the popularity of Bitcoin, the transfer of money in cryptocurrencies is becoming the latest trend now. The transfer of a monetary value in cryptocurrencies is not only easy but can also reduce third party fees. All the distributed ledger systems in cryptocurrencies are transparent and can save a lot of money, even big players such as private banks. Algorand and Gemini are some of the companies that are pioneering in this field of blockchain technology.

3. Changing the World With Smart Contracts

Smart contracts reduce a lot of middle men in any financial medium. Cryptocurrencies such as Ethereum and Cardano are based upon the philosophy of smart contracts and can add accountability to tons of decentralized financial applications in the future. Even governments, health care institutes, and real estate companies understand the benefits smart contracts offer and are almost ready to adopt this technology into real world use cases. Mediachain and Propy are some companies that are pioneering in providing innovative smart contracts technology to clients. Blockchain Technology for Personal Identity

Personal identity is an ongoing problem for millions of Americans and other citizens around the world. With blockchain technology, identity cannot be tampered with, and it will be virtually impossible to steal your identity. All the social security numbers, identification documents will be stored in the distributed ledger. Ligero, Civic, and Evernym are some companies using distributed ledger technology to create decentralized applications that can eliminate identity theft.

4. Blockchain Technology for Health Care

Blockchain technology provides a simple way to collect sensitive data from patients and use it for academic research without revealing the patient's identity. Blockchain technology can also extend to the health care system for reducing costs and managing employees effectively. All peer-reviewed research journals can also use Blockchain technology to cite only verified data. Wholesale and Patientory are few companies focusing on developing health care applications that utilize the prowess of blockchain technology.

5. Blockchain Technology for Logistics

With the growth of e-commerce, logistics has become an important part of the business. Logistics is, however, very crowded with different companies trying to prove their worth in the industry. There is also a problem with transparency due to a lack of communication in the logistics department of e-commerce companies. Customers also wish to know the whereabouts of their product without tampered or manipulated information.

Blockchain technology provides a reliable way to satisfy customer's and seller's needs by acknowledging different data sources and building trust. For example, if you wish to track a Walmart product, it would take more than two weeks to know about the product's producer. With blockchain technology, all your data will be available within a few seconds. DHL, Shipchain, and Maersk are some companies in the logistic space trying to implement blockchain technology in their services.

6. Art Collection With NFTs

Non-fungible tokens are right now the hottest blockchain application in 2021. NFTs are proving to be a great way of generating high value for both creators and investors. While there are many ways to streamline NFTs, right now, the most popular application is to help creators earn some additional bucks apart from their other revenue sources.

Candy, Dapper Labs, and Pixura are some startups trying to find innovative ways to utilize Non-fungible tokens with real estate and other real-world use cases.

7. Blockchain for Government

Even though Blockchain technology focuses on decentralization and is morally going in the opposite direction of government policies, governments can still use blockchain applications with centralization. For example, KYC compliance required to verify personal information can be made easier by using blockchain technology.

Issuing new citizenship, securing government documents, and providing transparency for citizens can also be made efficient by introducing government data into a blockchain platform. Using smart contracts to send pension amounts or special funds such as the Covid relief fund can be easily achieved with blockchain related monetary applications. Voatz and Follow my vote are some government projects that use blockchain technology to provide services for citizens.

8. Blockchain Technology for Media

Both multimedia and news outlets can use Blockchain technology to increase data privacy and provide royalties automatically. With Blockchain technology copyrighting or patenting your media can also become extremely easy. Blockchain technology can also offer a way to counter piracy and automatically delete them once a report is filed. Madhive, Steem, and Civil are companies that focus on developing decentralized applications that can revolutionize the media industry.

NFTs and Why They Are the Next Digital Revolution?

NFTs (Non-fungible Tokens) are the latest sensation in the cryptocurrency world. NFTs are being sold for millions of dollars, and many consider it a game-changer for collectors who use art as an investment choice. Recently, Twitter CEO Jack Dorsey sold his first tweet for three million dollars as an NFT. Non-fungible in NFT means that it is unique and cannot be replaced.

For example, an artwork produced by a renowned painter is non-fungible because it can exist in only one form. On the other hand, one USD or one BTC are fungible items because they are always equal to one of them and can be exchanged.

How Does an NFT Work?

NFTs represent ownership of a particular item. This item may be artwork, a music album cover, or even a website's domain name. Any item that needs proof of ownership can be issued as an NFT. NFTs are specifically designed to solve the problem of ownership when anyone can easily download a copy of the file. It isn't easy to track the file owner if it is easily available for everyone on the internet. NFTs are tokens that will live on the blockchain forever and represent your ownership until you sell it.

The digital artwork will usually be generated as a unique fingerprint and stored in the blockchain with a token name. An investor can now trade these tokens in several NFT bidding online platforms. No one can tamper with the token information as they are stored in the blockchain. NFT consists of all the previous owners of the token and how much they have spent on it.

Remember that when an investor owns an NFT, they will not get the physical copy of the item but its ownership. NFTs are usually hosted on the Ethereum platform, and anyone who is willing to sell their art as digital work needs to pay a gas fee to the Ethereum platform. NFTs are just in the beginning stage of their development, and their adaptation to other real-world use cases such as Real estate and domain names is still not satisfactory. Developers can also use smart contracts to create NFT supported applications in the decentralized finance domain to automatically send a part of the royalties whenever the item's ownership is changed.

ICOs and Future

Let us mention to you about ICOs with a simple example.

Tom is a businessman who wants to start a coffee shop in his surroundings. He has a great plan to make this coffee shop successful in his area. Now, three situations may happen.

1. **Tom Has Enough Money to Open a Coffee Shop**

Tom has saved enough money to open the coffee shop on his own. He uses this money to start a coffee shop and establishes a sole proprietorship of the business. Any losses or profits that occur in this business will belong entirely to Tom.

2. **Tom Doesn't Have Enough Money to Open a Coffee Shop**

Unfortunately, Tom doesn't have enough money to open a coffee shop, so he approaches Sam and Dom to help him. Sam and Dom provide the funds required for Tom, and they open a coffee shop. From a business perspective, Tom is the owner of the coffee shop, and Sam and Dom can be called venture capitalists. All the profits or losses will be shared between Tom, Sam, and Dom.

3. **Tom Is Unable to Raise the Capital Required**

The problem Tom faces here is that despite the contributions made by his friends Sam and Dom, he still does not have the essential capital to have the business up and running. To counter this problem, he starts to send invites to his neighbors and friends to contribute to his business. He mentions that this is a good investment choice and intrigues them about the business model. This is essentially an IPO or an ICO.

Here, all the neighbors that bought a part of TOM's business can be called shareholders.

ICOs (Initial Coin Offerings) are controversial in the crypto community and are banned in countries such as China due to the level of exploitation they have created in the initial years of their inception. ICOs are quite similar to IPOs, usually organized by companies that officially offer a part of their company to shareholders. The only difference between IPOs and ICOs is that IPOs are highly regulated, and it is difficult for a single individual to exploit their advantages.

On the other hand, ICOs are unregulated, and it is quite easy to create a white paper and raise money for unrealistic and unambitious projects. Even with all these disadvantages, ICOs can be considered a great way to invest as they provide higher returns, sometimes more than ten times the investment.

Different Countries and Regulations

Bitcoin, even though it has many advantages compared to fiat currencies, is considered controversial by many countries. China has been conservative about using cryptocurrencies as a transaction medium and has banned cryptocurrencies many years back. Even though China amounts to many retail investors and miners, Chinese authorities believe that it is a risk for their pegged currency yuan. Russia has also been quite strict about Bitcoin regulations.

The United States generally has a positive stance towards Bitcoin and has encouraged cryptocurrency investors to pay taxes. However, the IRS has mentioned that only less than 250 people have paid taxes citing Bitcoin as a revenue source.

Other countries such as Canada, New Zealand, Australia, and the European Union partially accept Bitcoin as a payment medium. In June 2021, El Salvador, a country in Central America, became the first country to accept Bitcoin as a legal tender.

Cryptocurrencies for Crime and Theft

Cryptocurrencies, mainly Bitcoin, are being rapidly used by criminals to make transactions in the darknet, which can be easily accessed using TOR software. The FBI has constantly expressed its concern over Bitcoin being used as an easy transaction medium by criminals. Law enforcement, financial regulators, and Wall Street big heads have also constantly pressurized the wrong impact of Bitcoin in its initial days. Due to its advantages, many people have changed their predictions about Bitcoin over time.

Bitcoin and other cryptocurrencies have their pros and cons, but the Blockchain technology that these cryptocurrencies rely on is a revolutionary technology that could change the way humans perceive financial institutions and transactions within the next few decades.

Chapter 7:

Cryptocurrency Risks

As with any financial instrument, cryptocurrencies have their own set of risks. Cryptocurrencies are right now considered high-risk instruments in the economic sphere. Understanding the different types of risks cryptocurrencies possess and finding a way to minimize them using risk management, and hedging techniques is an essential prerequisite for anyone serious about making profitable returns with cryptocurrencies.

What Is a Risk?

According to crypto terminology, risk is a monetary phenomenon where your initial capital investment can be lost entirely or decreased due to a decrease in the value of the financial instrument you invested in.

What Are the Risks of Cryptocurrencies?

1. Volatile

All cryptocurrencies are volatile financial instruments. Any sharp increase or decrease in the cryptocurrency value in a volatile market can decrease your overall asset value. If you have a vast portfolio, then your losses may be higher during a bear market.

2. Unregulated

As cryptocurrencies are decentralized networks, they are unregulated by the central authorities. Countries like China have constantly been trying to ban them and influence other countries to follow their path to protect their pegged currency yuan. While the United States government is optimistic about cryptocurrencies, it is still quite uncertain about their future—hence there are always regulation risks.

3. **Can Be Hacked**

Even though cryptocurrencies depend on the secured blockchain platform, there is a significant probability of your assets getting hacked or phished due to your negligence. Sometimes vulnerabilities in exchanges and blockchain platforms can also lead to your holdings being liquidated.

4. **Liquidity Risk**

Not all cryptocurrencies have a high liquidity ratio. Influential crypto investors can easily manipulate several altcoins. Many fall prey to the manipulated value of the altcoin leading to an increase in its value. Once the perpetrators get their desired value, they will slowly dump their holdings, leading to a sudden decrease in the value and liquidity of the cryptocurrency.

Risk Management

Anyone involved in crypto trading should not invest the amount they can afford to lose. When you invest in cryptocurrencies, you need to be as rational as possible. Risk management techniques can help investors not lose too much when the market moves opposite to their bet. Understanding some of the popular cryptocurrency risk management strategies can help investors to allocate their funds better.

Position Sizing

Usually, many beginners involved with crypto investing try to allocate their trading capital to a single cryptocurrency. For example, investing 100% of your trading capital in Ethereum only is a bad idea. You should never put all your eggs in one basket. Instead, invest 30% or less than your capital investment into a single cryptocurrency.

To achieve position sizing, a cryptocurrency investor can follow three popular strategies, as explained below.

Enter Amount vs. Risk Amount

In this strategy, an investor will not invest money that is more than the risk amount they can afford. For example, if your risk per trade is three percent, then an investor cannot trade any amount that is more than the risk amount according to this risk management strategy. You can further minimize your losses by using stop losses at a determined level.

Elder's "Sharks" and "Piranhas."

This is a position sizing strategy, where an investor needs to follow two strict rules. Dr. Alexander Elder introduces these rules for profitably diversifying financial instruments.

1. An investor should always limit his risk to 2%. Anything that is above 2% is not allowed and should be avoided by the investor. This is considered a shark bite by Elder as it is devastating and occurs all at one time for an investor.

2. An investor should always limit his risk to 6% per session. Anything above 6% is not allowed and should be avoided by the investor until the next trading session. This is considered a piranha attack because instead of giving a high loss like a shark bite, the losses are often more minor but continuous.

Kelly Criterion

The Kelly criterion is a formula that investors use to determine how much they should position their portfolio. Long-term traders usually follow the Kelly criterion.

Result = (Success % / Loss) - ((1- success %) / Take profit)

For example, using the Kelly criterion formula, for a stock size of $5000, an investor should not risk more than 19% of the entire capital. Kelly criterion is complex and involves many metrics such as Stop loss percentage and Take profit percentage to find a reliable position size percentage.

Risk / Reward Ratio

Every cryptocurrency is volatile and has a chance of either tanking or surging within very little time. Due to being a highly speculative market, crypto prices are usually not entirely dependent on fundamental analysis factors but depend on market psychology and forecast response.

A risk/reward ratio is usually used to estimate how much you can risk for a trade. Usually, a trade with huge risk always has the potential for a high reward. Knowing the risk/reward ratio can help investors to understand when to enter and exit the trade.

To calculate the risk-reward ratio, an investor needs to have entry and target price along with the stop-loss price.

Risk Reward Ratio = (Target - Entry) / (Entry - Stop loss)

Usually, it will be best if you never get involved in a trade that has a ratio lower than 1:1. Many traders, however, have a 1:1.5 ratio.

Utilizing Stop Losses and Take Profits

Stop losses and take profits are complex spot trading instruments that both day and position crypto traders can use to quickly sell or liquidate their positions whenever it reaches a specific price level. However, it needs to be remembered that both stop losses and take profits are not perfect, and there is no guarantee that they will work when there is high volatility or panic selling in the market.

Many crypto exchanges such as Binance and Coinbase provide trailing stop losses and take profits to participate in trades. When you use stop losses, your open positions will be closed when it reaches the price level below the barrier. Stop losses are great tools for crypto investors, especially during an aggressive bear market.

On the other hand, your open orders will be automatically liquidated when you use take profits instead of waiting to maximize your returns. Take profits are great tools for crypto investors, especially during a highly fluctuating market.

Hedging for Avoiding Cryptocurrency Risk

Hedging is a popular investment strategy that investors use to reduce the risk of open positions in their portfolios. In a hedging strategy, an investor usually involves one or more concurrent bets to minimize their losses. Hedging is first used by stock traders and is later popularised by bulls in the market during the housing bubble crisis that occurred in 2008. Hedging, even though minimizing your losses, also restricts your profits to a limited zone. In a highly fluctuated market with high uncertainty, it is better to proceed with fewer profits and minimize risks for not losing your capital investment within less time.

Investors investing in hedging strategies need to be entirely creative. The strategies we present now are the popular hedging strategies in the cryptocurrency market. To be a better investor, you need to apply hedging strategies using customized research and principles for your open positions.

1. Short Selling

Short selling is an investment strategy where an investor believes that there will be a decline in the asset price and decides to sell his open positions in the hope of repurchasing them at a lower price. Short sellers usually use technical analysis to determine when to sell a position and repurchase them.

You can use your short positions to hedge your long positions. Investors can use margin trading to trade more positions than they can actually afford using leverage options. Many investors also borrow open positions from their brokers to sell and buy them at lower prices and make a considerable profit. However, short selling is entirely risky and can extend your losses relatively if the value decreases drastically. Many brokers will automatically close your account if your trading account balance falls below the margin amount due to losses.

2. Futures

When you buy or sell a futures contract, you agree to sell or buy a particular asset at a specific time for a fixed price. Future contracts are also tradable assets and can be sold to other investors on a supported derivative exchange. Futures belong to a large category of financial instruments, which are known as derivatives. Derivatives are tradable assets that depend on the underlying value of another asset.

An investor can use future contracts to hedge an open position. However, remember that if a cryptocurrency fluctuates highly, you may need to face huge losses. You are obligated to buy or sell cryptocurrencies when you buy a futures contract according to the agreement conditions. If not, you may be legally sued by the other party involved in the transaction. Several decentralized financial applications are being developed to create an easy way to exchange future contracts using an escrow-based service.

3. Options

Options are similar to futures and belong to the derivatives category. While when you buy a futures contract, you are obligated to fulfill the contract. On the other hand, when you buy an option contract, you will have a choice to exercise or not. This choice is very powerful, especially when you lose the bet. To buy an option contract, you need to pay a premium.

You can exercise different options contracts and either buy or sell cryptocurrencies at an agreed-upon price.

Chapter 8:

Money Management And Saving

For an individual to be a successful investor, they must first grasp the essence of money. Money management is the process of managing, growing, and saving money so that one can become financially independent. Money management principles can help traders manage their portfolios from a financial standpoint. In markets such as the cryptocurrency realm, where volatility is high, individuals need to abide by a strict set of rules for managing their money.

How to Save Money?

The concept of saving money is often misunderstood despite its simplicity. In the world of rising living costs, there needs to be an incentive to save money and increase its value over time.

To save money, you need to limit your costs by maintaining a strict budget. You can effectively save money by constantly tracking your expenses and taxes using both mobile and desktop apps. A budget tracking system can help you find the errors in your allocation of budget money quickly, eliminating the temptation to make impulse purchases.

Paying your credit card bills on time and opening a savings account to receive short interest can also be a great way to save money.

How to Grow Money?

It is everyone's dream to be able to exponentially increase the value of their savings. It is advisable to follow some of the listed rules so that you can increase your money at a more reasonable pace.

1. Never Get Into Debt.

In addition to reducing your financial independence, debts can be very demotivating. While it is entirely okay to get into debts for a business or a college education, you, however, need to make sure that you will be able to clear them as soon as possible. Not paying debts on time can lead to both physical and emotional stress. Getting rid of debt as quickly as possible will greatly contribute to the improvement of your financial prospects.

2. Be Consistent With Your Investments.

To grow money consistently, you need to be consistent with your investments without deviating from your financial goals. By taking part in an investment strategy, you can utilize principles such as rupee cost averaging and compound interest to grow your money.

3. Always Diversify

Make sure that your savings are diversified to ensure that you receive guaranteed returns. For example, if you invest in similar assets, then there is a chance for your portfolio to become invaluable with the wrong estimation. Invest in non-similar assets and give them some time to let them grow in value.

Money Management Techniques

Money management is an art, and everyone has their technique to manage their wealth and let it grow in value.

1. Understand Your Current Position

For any money management technique to be effective, you need first to analyze your financial position. Look at your income, credit reports, loans, debts, and credit card payments to estimate your savings. If you are unaware of analysis techniques, contact a professional to show a report of your financial position. Knowing your position financially can make you reduce your expenses and focus on investing them in different financial instruments. Make both minor and significant goals to keep you motivated and not get too comfortable with small returns.

2. Form an Emergency Fund

While it is true that you have to satisfy some of your luxuries to invest in financial instruments, you, however, should never invest money that is important for emergency purposes. Maintain an emergency fund to face any hurdles that occur in life. Nothing is more painful than having to liquidate a financial instrument at a loss.

3. Make Sure That You Are Saving for Retirement

Retiring is scary and is often less overlooked by both employers and employees. Investing in retirement accounts can be easier with the assistance of tax exemptions and policies offered by governments. Retirement savings can be viewed as a strategy for effective money management over a longer period of time.

4. **Record Paperwork**

Make sure that you are filing paperwork for your expenses in an organized way. Being organized can help you to file taxes easily and estimate your costs and profits or losses for a financial year. There are several online tools to easily save your receipts, paperwork, and agreement with a high-level encryption mechanism.

Understanding Online Banking

A few decades back, all financial transactions were usually made through banks located in different outlets. With the revolution of accessible internet and banking technology, we can make our bank transactions using an online account. With an online bank account, you don't need to visit a bank branch for every minor transaction but can make them through services such as Internet Banking or Mobile app banking.

What Do You Need?

To open an Online banking account, you typically need a bank account from any private or public bank. To avoid confusion, you need first to create a standard bank account from your bank branch and can instantly convert it to an online bank account with a few steps of verification, such as completing KYC compliance and activating two-factor authentication.

Once these details are provided, your online ledger will be created, providing you with the ability to deposit money or withdraw it quickly. You can contact bank representatives to receive credit cards, debit cards, or access internet banking.

Time, Patience, and Persistence For Investors

As an investor, you need to focus on time, patience, and persistence to succeed in the long run. While they may seem like simple behavioral concepts, a successful investor needs to master different skills that surround these principles to grow consistently in the market.

Time

Time is the biggest asset that an individual often neglects. With time, you can either attain financial independence or get yourself filled with debts. Time is a valuable resource an investor needs to know how to spend. As an investor, you also need to follow certain time management principles such as a Pomodoro technique while performing trading disciplines such as fundamental and technical analysis for your trades.

How to Utilize Your Time Perfectly?

1. Follow techniques such as setting reminders, establishing a routine, and blocking distractions to improve your investing workflow.
2. Maintain strict trading times if you are a cryptocurrency investor.
3. If you are a day trader or a scalper, use Pareto analysis to streamline your trade executions.

4. Master advanced techniques such as the Eisenhower Matrix, Parkinson's law, and the time blocking method to divide your time if you are a technical analyst.

5. Follow the Getting Things Done (GTD) method if you are a fundamental analyst overwhelmed by the high amount of research.

6. Spare a specific time in a day for skimming over Blog posts, social media interactions, and forums related to your cryptocurrency portfolio.

Patience

Patience is not a skill but a lifestyle for many individuals. Having patience can transform careers and personal relationships. As an investor, you need to be patient, especially when there is volatility that leads to panic in the market. To achieve patience, we recommend you to follow the below-mentioned principles.

- Practice meditation and yoga for controlling your negative thoughts
- Have a clear plan for all your trades
- Either take a vacation or learn a hobby to get rid of stress
- Practice being patient. Make it a habit.

Persistence

Markets, especially the cryptocurrency market, are volatile and make investors lose their confidence because of a market crash. To have consistent and profitable returns, an investor needs to be persistent about his decision. To be persistent with an investment decision, individuals need to be highly confident about their fundamental and technical skills. To be persistent, first, improve your skills in the market and make yourselves believe that your prediction will be correct.

Chapter 9:

Everything about altcoins

Bitcoin has been ruling the cryptocurrency market right from its inception in 2009. In 2021, Bitcoin occupies more than 80% of the net worth of all the available cryptocurrencies. Even though Bitcoin is a widely accepted cryptocurrency, it is not considered a favorable investment option by many individuals. Even though being volatile and unpredictable, the price of Bitcoin is high for a retail investor. For an investor who is enthusiastic and optimistic about the essence of the crypto industry, learning about altcoins is essential.

Why Are Altcoins Vital?

Altcoins are cryptocurrencies that are alternatives to Bitcoin. The most popular altcoin is Ethereum and has the second-largest market capitalization of all cryptocurrencies that exist out there. Most of the altcoins follow the decentralized principles that Bitcoin believes in. While Bitcoin is considered as a more standard currency that can be used as an exchange or storage value, altcoins focus on empowering the essence of blockchain technology in the real world.

How to Invest in Altcoins?

There is a lot of money to be made in the alternative cryptocurrency market. According to the coin market cap, in the second half of 2021, altcoins account for 45% of the cryptocurrency market. Altcoins are highly influential on the Bitcoin price trajectory most of the time. So, to invest in altcoins, you first need to understand the philosophy of Bitcoin and Blockchain technology.

1. **Do Research**

To invest in any altcoins, you need first to do sufficient research about the cryptocurrency. The users of new high-performing altcoins are usually manipulated by the bag holders. Before deciding whether or not to invest in an altcoin, you need first to read its white paper and the problem it is trying to solve in the crypto world. Your research should focus on different factors such as market capitalization, consensus algorithm, and level of decentralization.

2. **Understand Volatility and Liquidity**

To understand whether or not an altcoin is a better investment, you need to watch the historical chart of the altcoin volatility. If there is a constant fluctuation in prices, then it may not be a great investment choice.

Liquidity refers to how easy it is to buy or sell an altcoin to fiat currency or the US pegged cryptocurrencies. If there is less liquidity, it becomes challenging to liquidate your position, especially when there is panic selling. As all altcoins are subject to fraud and dumping, you need to ensure that the liquidity is satisfactory before investing.

3. **Diversify Your Investment**

As altcoins are usually highly volatile, you need to diversify your investment in more altcoins. For example, investing $1000 in Ethereum, Litecoin, Cardano, Stellar, and Chain Link combined is less risky than investing $1000 in Ethereum itself. To prioritize which altcoins more while diversifying your funds, use an accumulation strategy. Read peer-reviewed journals and trade magazines to estimate an altcoin future and decide on what you are going to invest more.

4. Do Not Get Stuck

Not all altcoins have a future. Unlike stocks, altcoins can lose their value pretty quickly. To not live with invaluable positions, make sure that you exit from the game with triggering signals. Unlike Bitcoin, altcoins are not a fixed asset that crypto investors depend upon. For example, if a service that provides much more reliable data than Chain Link comes into the cryptocurrency market, then the value and market capitalization of Chain Link will decrease instantly. Just like any market, the cryptocurrency market too follows supply and demand. Make sure that you are investing in altcoins that have high demand and less supply.

Note: Never invest in cryptocurrency coins such as Dogecoin, which has an unlimited supply of coins. They are often referred to as "shitcoins" by the crypto community due to their manipulated value in the market.

Ethereum and Its Importance

Ethereum is the second most popular cryptocurrency right now. While Bitcoin is primarily used as a store of value, Ethereum provides a way to develop decentralized applications and services in the blockchain system. Ethereum focuses on decentralizing the internet with the implementation of smart contracts in its blockchain platform.

How Does Ethereum Work?

For example, take your smartphone and visit the App Store if you have an Apple device or Google Play Store if you have an Android device. Now, you will see different types of apps that can work for your mobile device. Apps listed in the AppStore will not work on an Android device and vice versa.

The Ethereum blockchain acts as a platform for developers willing to provide applications based on blockchain technology. These apps are known as decentralized applications and are charged by the Ethereum platform in gas fees based on the number of transactions.

How Do These Decentralized Applications Work?

Decentralized applications usually depend on smart contracts to solve real-world problems. Smart contracts are pretty common to contracts in the real world but are entirely digital. All the smart contracts created for an Ethereum Dapp will be stored on the Ethereum blockchain.

How Do Smart Contracts Work?

To understand how smart contracts work, you need to know how Kickstarter works. Kickstarter is a third party that sits between the developers and supporters in a crowdfunding program. Kickstarter will release funds to the developers from the collected money only when a milestone is achieved.

In the above scenario, Kickstarter is a third party that consists of humans who verify the authenticity of the project development. Smart contracts, however, use programming to make everything become automatic. Ethereum uses smart contracts written in a programming language known as Solidity, developed explicitly for Ethereum.

The only difference between Kickstarter and smart contracts is that all the properties are stored on the blockchain, and hence it becomes difficult for anyone to change or modify the smart contract once it is written. The immutable and distributed nature of smart contacts has made them more reliable among blockchain users.

Some Real-Life Examples:

1. Banks can use smart contracts to send automatic interest payments for their account holders.

2. Insurance companies can process claims automatically

3. Logistic companies can automatically get paid when a particular product is delivered.

Cardano and Its Importance

Cardano is a blockchain platform that uses smart contracts to create decentralized applications. The significant difference between Cardano and other blockchain platforms is that it is entirely peer-reviewed, and every update is backed by academic research. Cardano uses a proof of stake algorithm to validate the transactions.

Cardano uses programming languages, Plautus and Marlowe, to create high-level financial smart contracts.

How Does Proof of Stake Work?

In the famous proof of work algorithm, the nodes need to solve complex mathematical problems using high energy. Proof of stake relies entirely on a random election process that decides which node must verify a block based on various factors. Cardano uses advanced algorithmic principles to make sure that not only a few nodes get elected every time.

1. A node first needs to buy cryptocurrency tokens ($ADA) and wait for their chance to mine a block.

2. If a node gets selected, then the system will stake a part of his wealth, and the node will verify the blocks using specific software.

3. Once the verification is completed, the node will wait for other nodes to confirm the transaction, and once it receives their consensus, the block will be added to the blockchain.

4. The staked amount and the reward earned will be released to the node's account after some time.

Ouroboros is a new set of cryptographic principles that Cardano's proof of stake algorithm uses to select nodes and verify the transactions.

Polkadot and Its Importance

Polkadot focuses on protocol limitations of blockchains that can cause bottleneck situations when there are a high number of transactions. When a bottleneck occurs, the transaction fees will increase, or the blockchain may go offline. Ethereum faced this kind of bottleneck situation when a decentralized software known as Cryptokitties became extremely popular in the crypto community. In the world of NFTs, ICOs, and decentralized finance applications, having reliable blockchain platforms that battle these limitations is a god saver. Polkadot is one of those blockchains that assures better scalability and reliability using its relay par chains.

How Does Polkadot Work?

In a Polkadot relay chain, all individual blockchains will be connected like spokes are connected to the hub of a wheel. All the blockchains connected to this relay chain have different purposes and can be easily optimized. Developers can use this to program or make updates to the blockchain easily. Relay chain provides an easy way to communicate between each other and improves scalability. All the blockchains connected to the relay chain are known as para chains and allow the transfer of any data between each other.

With Polkadot, it becomes easier to update blockchains and create decentralized applications with complex functionalities. Polkadot uses the Proof of stake algorithm as its consensus mechanism.

Chain Link and Its Importance

Smart contracts are arguably the most popular innovation in blockchain technology. They eliminate third parties by automatically triggering events whenever a particular milestone is reached.

For example, if you want to transfer five BTC whenever your crypto wallet becomes zero, you can easily do it using a smart contract. However, real-world applications with smart contracts need to interact with reliable data feeds to make decisions. For example, a decentralized sports betting platform needs data about live events to trigger actions. Chain Link solves this problem and provides reliable data feeds to developers focusing on developing decentralized applications of different kinds.

Chain Link consists of Oracles that collect live data and send them to decentralized applications whenever certain information is needed. All these Oracles receive rewards in the form of a LINK token whenever they are called by the application. Chain Link also penalizes data providers who provide consistently incorrect information. Many Ethereum supported decentralized finance applications depend on Chain Link to provide reliable price changes of different financial instruments.

Litecoin and Its Importance

While Bitcoin is called digital gold, Litecoin is called digital silver by crypto enthusiasts. Charlie Lee created Litecoin in 2011 as a lighter version of Bitcoin. Charlie Lee has mentioned several times that his aim to create Litecoin is not to be an alternative to Bitcoin but to be used along with Bitcoin. Litecoin is a decentralized cryptocurrency that improves mining speed and provides faster transactions than Bitcoin.

With Litecoin, miners who validate and add transactions to the distributed ledger system get an easier way to make the validation. All Litecoin transactions will be added within 2.5 minutes instead of the 10 minutes required for Bitcoin. Litecoin is also very liberal about introducing new technologies into its blockchain platform. For example, in 2017, Litecoin became the first cryptocurrency to implement lightning network transactions.

Litecoin also uses the Scrypt cryptographic algorithm instead of the SHA-256 hashing algorithm that Bitcoin uses. Scrypt is less complex than SHA-256 and allows miners to mine LTC using graphic cards such as NVIDIA.

Ripple and Its Importance

Ripple is a centralized Blockchain network that focuses on providing instant transactions for big players such as financial institutions, central and private banks. Ripple is a revolutionary approach to the blockchain network and is considered an ambitious project by many crypto experts.

Why Is Ripple Necessary?

Ripple is necessary for foreign transactions where there is no structural development in the last twenty years, even with the rapid advancement of the internet. The reason for the delay in foreign transactions is due to different protocols countries use for their transactions.

Ripple solves this problem by creating a network known as RippleNet, which can make transactions within a few seconds.

What Happens in a Ripple Net Transaction?

1. The sender will convert Fiat currency into Ripple XRP. A Sender should usually add a transaction fee that Ripple charges to the amount for being transparent with the receiver. A sender should mention the receiver's ripple address to make an instant transaction.

2. Once the currency is converted into XRP, it will be sent to the receiver's address, and the receiver can exchange it for fiat currency using one of the UNL nodes that act as a validator on the Ripple Net blockchain.

In order to make crypto to fiat conversions as easy as possible, Ripple has made agreements with hundreds of payment providers. XRP is the native token of Ripple and is right now the third most popular cryptocurrency according to market capitalization.

Chapter 10:

Cryptocurrencies Vs Stocks

Even though cryptocurrency is the latest sensation in the financial sphere, stock markets have always given investors consistent returns. Stocks and cryptocurrencies are both different worlds. Both investors involved in these financial instruments, however, have a common goal, which is profits. Understanding what stocks are and how they work can help a crypto investor appreciate the actual value of cryptocurrencies.

Understanding the Stock Market

Stock markets are arguably the most popular financial markets in the world. Investors in the stock market are usually conservative and depend on the popular buy-and-hold method to increase the value of their portfolios. When you buy stock in a company, you represent ownership in a company or a firm. While this ownership may seem negligible from the bigger picture, you still have your ownership rights and can sometimes influence the company's policies by voicing your disappointment.

What Is a Stock?

A stock is a financial instrument that represents a part of a company's equity. Stock value usually increases depending on supply and demand. A public trading company usually needs to release its earnings reports every quarter. According to these reports, if the company is making profits, then the demand for the shares increases, making your stock value surge. Similarly, if a company is making losses or receiving bad media attention, then the value of the stock will plummet.

Companies usually make their company public when they need additional capital to improve their infrastructure and improve their products or services. As the business expands, capital requirements increase, making dependence on venture capitalists tough. When a company decides to go public, it first releases an IPO (Initial public offering) to sell its initial shares to investors.

Once an IPO is completed, the company will be listed on all public exchanges such as the NYSE. A stock exchange is a secondary market where buyers and sellers meet to exchange their shares. However, remember that not all stocks are listed on the public exchanges due to regulations. Some small and international companies will usually be traded using OTC (over-the-counter) exchanges.

Most of the developing and developed countries use stock exchanges to stabilize their economy. A consistent bull run in the stock markets will lead to a prosperous economy, and a bear run in the stock markets usually will lead to recession.

How to Invest in Stocks?

There are several ways to invest in stocks. Knowing different strategies can help you to become innovative while trading in the stock market.

1. **Using Online Brokers**

Using online brokers, an investor can participate in all kinds of trading practices. For example, you can easily short positions to make some quick bucks. Brokers also provide leverage options to increase your profits.

What Is Leverage?

Leverage is a monetary model in which a broker lets you trade with money more than you hold in your trading account. Usually, brokers offer a 1:10 leverage ratio for beginners. If you have $1000 in your trading account, you can bet positions that value $10000. Depending on their past performance and credit score, more experienced traders will also receive up to a 1: 100 leverage ratio.

Leverage is an extremely risky financial instrument that can make you lose all the money in your trading account with a few bad trades. Use leverage only when you are confident about your trading decision.

2. Using Robo Advisers

Many investors currently depend on artificial robot advisors that can analyze market trends and provide investment advice. Robo advisors usually use complex artificial intelligence and machine learning algorithms to find patterns in the market trends. Using Robo advisors along with professional broker advice can be a great way to maximize your profits.

3. Using Mutual Funds

If you are not interested in investing in just one company, you can join a mutual fund pool to diversify your investment across various companies. Mutual funds also provide consistent profits as they are usually managed by a technically sound fund manager who does the research and fundamental analysis for you.

How Are Stocks Different From Cryptocurrencies?

Even though stocks are less volatile than cryptocurrencies, they, however, provide fewer returns than cryptocurrencies. Cryptocurrencies are more volatile and offer returns that are usually very high. For example if you invested in Bitcoin a decade back, your asset value now would be ten thousand times more than your initial investment. Knowing some of the differences between stocks and cryptocurrencies is vital for an average investor.

1. Volatility and Liquidity

The volatility and liquidity for stocks are much better than for cryptocurrencies. All public trading companies are usually regulated and are constantly monitored by governments not to disrupt the monetary condition of the economy. Cryptocurrencies, on the other hand, provide privacy and are challenging to monitor. Even governments do not bother themselves with monitoring even popular cryptocurrencies because it requires a lot of resources. Due to this sole reason, cryptocurrencies are usually difficult to be trusted, increasing volatility and a decrease in liquidity.

2. Returns

No other financial instrument provides as high returns as cryptocurrencies. A popular growth stock only provides 10% of the profits a growth cryptocurrency offers. However, it would be best to remember that cryptocurrencies are also high-risk instruments than stocks and can make you lose all your initial capital within less time.

3. Large Diversity

Both stocks and cryptocurrencies provide extensive, diverse options for all investors. For example, on stock markets, you can find companies related to different sectors. On the other hand, there are cryptocurrencies pertaining to various sectors but they are still not as popular as public traded companies.

Advantages of Stocks

1. Gains

Even though there is a problem with short-term fluctuations, stocks have a history of providing higher returns for patient investors. Almost all value stocks have provided more than five-time returns for investors who have bought them in their initial phases. To have more gains, efficient fundamental research on sectors and companies is essential.

2. Drives a Growing Economy

When you invest in a public traded company, you essentially believe that a company can perform better in the present conditions. When you help a company secure its capital, you are effectively helping that company to stay in the race and create new products and services that can increase its capital revenue and drive the economy. Investing in stocks can help you understand different business cycle phases, such as peak, contraction, and trough.

3. Beat inflation

Inflation is an economic concept that every investor needs to be aware of, especially when thinking of a long-term investment.

Usually, currency value decreases as time passes due to changes in both economic and financial indicators. Stocks have a history of providing higher inflation yields than other financial instruments.

4. Dividends

Stocks provide a consistent yearly income known as dividends. Dividends are usually offered by value companies such as Apple but not by growth companies such as Tesla. Understanding dividend yield rates and how you can improve your dividend returns is a great way to understand market dynamics.

Disadvantages of Stocks

1. Risky

Stock markets are inherently risky as many factors decide the market movement. When trading in the stock market, you will observe that the market prices will change more often, not due to reports but due to investors' speculation. Market psychology and forecasts hold a strong influence in deciding the price of stocks. If there is a panic or less confidence in a company, then the stockholders will start to sell the shares making the prices of stocks plummet.

2. Problems of Bankruptcy

Sometimes public traded companies may declare bankruptcy due to considerable losses in a quarter or due to competitors rising above them and occupying their market share. When a publicly traded company declares bankruptcy, stockholders are the last priority for the IRS to clear losses.

3. **Requires High Knowledge**

Investing in stocks without a rigorous fundamental analysis or technical analysis is a bad idea. All stockholders should do their research or depend on a highly qualified broker to make their trading decisions. Otherwise, it isn't easy to maintain consistent profits in the ever-evolving market.

Investing in Both Stocks and Cryptocurrencies

To allocate your capital efficiently, we suggest you invest in both stocks and cryptocurrencies simultaneously. By investing in two different financial instruments, you will be diversifying your portfolio. Stocks are usually dependent on various factors such as politics, economics, and earnings reports. On the other hand, cryptocurrencies are entirely dependent on speculators' confidence in the concept of decentralization.

We recommend placing 60% of your portfolio in cryptocurrencies and 40% in stocks for better results. Diversifying your portfolio with other financial instruments such as mutual funds, real estate, ETFs, and CDs is also a recommended path for better returns.

Different Types of Traders in the Financial Market

Day Trader

A day trader observes the short-term market fluctuations and bets the market after carefully following technical analysis trends. For a day trader, volatility is the key to making profits or facing losses. Day traders use technical indicators such as the MACD indicator to detect patterns that can help them estimate the asset price movement. Day traders don't depend on fundamental analysis factors while trading. Most of the trades in a cryptocurrency market are speculative, and hence it becomes easy to determine patterns as the market usually repeats itself. A day trader usually closes his open positions within 24 hours. Several brokers provide spot and peer-to-peer trading services to traders.

For day traders, investing in altcoins is a great way to make some quick profits. Many day traders don't believe in trading with popular cryptocurrencies such as Bitcoin and Ethereum, as they are primarily unpredictable using technical analysis techniques.

1. *Swing Trader*

A swing trader uses the same principles as a day trader but extends their trading time from 24 hours to a few days or weeks. A swing trader relies on both fundamental and technical analysis techniques to make their trading decisions. Swing traders observe for swings usually formed due to big market players' constant dumping and pumping of cryptocurrencies. Swing traders sole focus is to spot these swings on technical charts and find out when to enter or exit the trade. Spotting swings needs extreme observation skills and a bit of patience.

While swing traders are pretty popular in the stock markets, finding them in the cryptocurrency arena is challenging as fewer big market players occupy the crypto world. Hence, it becomes difficult to spot swings in the over-speculative market.

2. Position Trader

Position traders are classic investors who buy an asset and forget about it for many years. Position traders usually need to invest in money that they can afford to lose. However, a position trader should constantly be observing the news and social media to judge that their investment is a good bet. Position traders need extreme patience as they should not worry about short-term price fluctuations and aggressive bear markets.

As a position trader, you need to make sure that your investment is a good choice by cross-checking with different brokers and by your own research.

3. Reverse Trader

A reverse trader is someone who makes trading decisions opposite to the market sentiment. Reverse traders will usually analyze market forecast reports. They will observe the investor's sentiment over a particular asset over time and decide precisely opposite to the popular choice. Reverse traders believe that there is always a chance to grow in a crisis. Many reverse traders will buy the dip when the market is falling and will wait for the market to grow.

4. Derivatives Trader

A derivative trader usually trades or hedges their open positions using derivatives such as futures, forwards, and options. Unlike the stock market, the derivatives market is significantly less in the cryptocurrency market. Derivatives are not popular due to high volatility in the cryptocurrency market.

To succeed as a derivative trader, you need to first understand the philosophy of the derivatives and trade only with higher expiration dates instead of buying contracts with less expiration dates.

5. Scalper

A scalper is a trader who usually utilizes the small market movements in the market. They entirely depend on technical analysis and will constantly be involved in trades whenever there is a rise in the asset price. As scalpers are engaged in many trades, they usually need to open an account with a broker who offers flat commission rates and high leverage rates for cryptocurrency investors.

Conclusion

To succeed in investing, an individual needs to first be thorough with the basics and judge a financial instrument without any bias. This book focused on providing accurate information that can be a gold mine for beginners looking forward to becoming a part of the speculation involved in the cryptocurrency market. First of all, congrats on completing the book with determination. With the consumed information, you are now all set to test your bets regarding the asset price movement in the cryptocurrency market.

For a cryptocurrency investor, it is essential to follow some of the traits that are said to be successful with several cryptocurrency investors.

Character Traits for Cryptocurrency Investors

1. Goal Setting

Goal setting is vital for any investor. Having clear goals and creating different plans to reach these goals is essential for an investor. Investors can approach goals with different strategies, but ultimately a disciplined investor will always focus on his goals at the end. Having realistic goals can also help investors face the uncertainty that is very common in the cryptocurrency market.

We recommend using to-do list apps and mind-maps to create different approaches to your goals.

2. Knowledge Is Power

For an investor in the cryptocurrency market, knowledge is essential to judge when to enter and exit the trade. Unlike other financial markets, cryptocurrencies are decentralized, and hence the knowledge regarding these assets is usually manipulated. To find reliable information, you need only to approach the official website of the blockchain platform. Reading peer-reviewed journals and trade magazines can also help you better understand the market from a bigger picture. To be successful in the market, an investor should always anticipate acquiring knowledge from different sources and mediums.

3. Judge Decisions

There are many sheep in the cryptocurrency market who are always inclined to follow other's trade decisions instead of depending on their research. While it is essential to follow influencers to understand market sentiment, you should never believe anyone's words to make your financial decisions. Never join the bandwagon just because everyone else is doing it. Be rational and stop being greedy to have a future in the cryptocurrency market.

4. Achieve Patience

To become a successful investor, patience is crucial. With patience, you will not make decisions that can reduce your portfolio value. Successful investors will always stick to the plan and make sure that they achieve their goals. With patience, investors can avoid bad practices such as panic selling and revenge trading.

5. Choose Between Gut and Research

As an investor, you need to often choose between your gut and research while making decisions. As a beginner, we, however, suggest you blindly trust your research. However, when you gain experience, it is vital to listen to your gut for making trading decisions.

6. Maintain a Trading Journal

Always journal your trading practices in general. Introspecting your decisions and looking out both at your success and failures in investing in written form can be a great motivation during future trades.

We hope that you will have fun trading in the cryptocurrency market. Happy investing!

Disclaimer:

This book is a guide written for beginners to understand the basics of the ever-expanding cryptocurrency market. The book's author is not responsible for any financial decisions made by the reader of the book. Cryptocurrency is a highly volatile market, and anyone looking forward to investing in the market should do their research and invest only what they can afford to lose.

References

Bernard Marr. *What is the difference between Bitcoin and Ripple?* (n.d.). Bernard Marr. https://bernardmarr.com/default.asp?contentID=1384

Blockchain Explained: What is blockchain? (n.d.). Euromoney Learning. https://www.euromoney.com/learning/blockchain-explained/what-is-blockchain

Frankenfield, J. (2021, February 18). *Bitcoin.* Investopedia. https://www.investopedia.com/terms/b/bitcoin.asp

What is Ethereum: Understanding its features and applications. (n.d.). Simplilearn. https://www.simplilearn.com/tutorials/blockchain-tutorial/what-is-ethereum

What is Cardano blockchain? [The most comprehensive step-by-step guide]. (2018, February 21). Blockgeeks. https://blockgeeks.com/guides/what-is-cardano/

Wood, G. (2021, May 17). *The launch of parachains.* Medium. https://medium.com/polkadot-network/the-launch-of-parachains-78188fcf024f

What are the risks? (n.d.). CMC Markets. https://www.cmcmarkets.com/en/learn-cryptocurrencies/what-are-the-risks

A guide to cryptocurrency fundamental analysis. (n.d.). Binance Academy. https://academy.binance.com/en/articles/a-guide-to-cryptocurrency-fundamental-analysis

Printed in Great Britain
by Amazon